# THE MAKING OF A NOVELIST

Novels by Margaret Thomson Davis:

*The Breadmakers*
*A Baby Might Be Crying*
*A Sort of Peace*
*The Prisoner*
*The Prince and the Tobacco Lords*
*Roots of Bondage*
*Scorpion in the Fire*
*The Dark Side of Pleasure*

# The Making
# of a
# Novelist

## MARGARET THOMSON DAVIS

ALLISON & BUSBY
LONDON

First published 1982 by
Allison and Busby Limited
6a Noel Street, London, W1V 3RB

British Library Cataloguing in Publication Data
Davis, Margaret Thomson
    The making of a novelist
    1.  Davis, Margaret Thomson
    2.  Authors, Scottish – 20th century – Biography
    I.  Title
    823.914      PR6054.A8926

ISBN 0-85031-434-8

Set in 10/11 pt Baskerville
by Alan Sutton Publishing Ltd, Gloucester
and printed in Great Britain by
The Camelot Press, Southampton

In loving memory of my mother
Christina Thomson

# CHAPTER ONE

FOR YEARS I thought my father was Robinson Crusoe. Then it began to dawn on me that I had been mistaken. He was, in fact, Jim Hawkins who had sailed in the good ship *Hispaniola*.

Every night my father told me stories of his adventures. Not for me the carefully chosen, gentle tales of Noddy or Peter Rabbit or Jemima Puddleduck to lull me into a safe, contented, dream-free sleep. As well as stories like *Robinson Crusoe* and *Treasure Island* my father told me, in a voice husky with drama and feeling, terrible tales of Sweeney Todd the demon barber. And Maria Marten and the murder in the Red Barn. And Burke and Hare the body-snatchers.

He related all the stories in the first person and acted them out with fiendish glee. At Christmas he was old Scrooge, and the ghosts of Christmas past, present and future, and Marlowe, all with different ghostly, blood-chilling voices. At Christmas he was also Santa Claus and out of the darkness of my bedroom would come his voice accompanied by a tinkling sound.

"Listen to the sleighbells," he'd hoarsely whisper. "Listen to them coming nearer and nearer!"

I knew that he was hiding behind the door clinking teaspoons together but I never had the heart to tell him I knew. He was having such a marvellous time.

Mostly, though, he swept me away with him to his make-believe land. I'll never forget the look of astonishment and fear on his face — emotions that were immediately mirrored in mine — when he told me that he'd spied the footprint in the sand. I was there, trembling in apprehension beside him every step of the way as he followed the footprints along the deserted beach. It was almost as terrifying as that time on the *Hispaniola* when we crouched down in the apple-barrel and listened to Long John Silver and watched Silver's knife hovering above our heads. There has never been anything quite so dramatic or vivid or exciting in my life as that moment.

I can still see my father's florid face and huge dark eyes and grey hair cut short and sticking straight up like a wire rug from his scalp. And I can hear his deep, rich voice singing, "Fifteen men on a dead man's chest! Yo, ho, ho, and a bottle of rum!"

All this is no doubt enough to give any child psychologist night-

1

mares but it enlarged, coloured, heightened my emotions, my sensitivity and my imagination. Most writers I have read about have had someone in their childhood who told them stories in this vivid and dramatic way.

Take Oliver Goldsmith for instance. His first teacher was a very eccentric, romantic type called Tom Byrne who was well versed in the fairy superstitions of the country. In school he often didn't feel like teaching a lesson and just told a story instead. Young Goldsmith's imagination appears to have been much excited by this man's stories. The books from which he learned to read were considered most unsuitable and shocked many people of his time. They were the penny-dreadfuls of the eighteenth century. Books like *A History of the Irish Rogues and Rapparees; The Lives of Celebrated Pirates; Moll Flanders; Jack, the Bachelor, the notorious smuggler* and *The Life and Adventures of James Fency, the Irish Robber.*

When Sir Walter Scott was a child his Aunt Janet read him ballads. His grandmother told him of border affairs. His uncle thrilled him with exciting stories about the campaigns of the American War of Independence. His brother, who was in the navy, kept him spellbound with stories of hairbreadth escapes and blood-curdling adventures.

Robert Louis Stevenson's father had a romantic imagination and kept his son entertained nightly with tales of ships, roadside inns, robbers and old sailors.

The child's nannie, Alison Cunningham or Cummie, had a strong imagination and a great love of rhetoric and dramatic speech.

"It's you that gave me a passion for the drama, Cummie," Louis told her on the last occasion they met.

"Me, Master Lou?" she replied. "I never put foot inside a playhouse in my life."

"Ay, woman," said Louis. "But it was the grand, dramatic way ye had of reciting the hymns."

Robert Burns was also told stirring tales on winters' nights, tales of witches and ghosties and fairies, when he was a child.

D.H. Lawrence's father could barely sign his name and could only painfully read the daily newspaper. His life and his attitude to life was primitive and almost entirely animal. Yet the artist's temperament that D.H. Lawrence inherited came from him and not his wife, for all her better education and her nagging sense of superiority.

Lawrence's father was a good dancer. At one time he even ran a dancing class. He told vivid stories to D.H. Lawrence about the countryside and about animals while out walking with him. This feeling for nature is reflected in much of Lawrence's work.

2

The list is endless.

This early stimulation of the imagination, this heightening of the sensitivity and the emotions, is the most important influence in a writer's life. You may well be a happier, more secure and contented child without all this stirring of the emotions but you'd have much less chance of becoming a creative writer.

Not that I ever in my wildest flights of fancy as a child or young adult, imagined that I could become a writer. Despite the power of my father's imagination such an audacious idea was completely beyond him as well. Writers were a different breed from us. They lived in a different world. Indeed it was hard to imagine that such creatures existed in flesh and blood at all. They were so far removed from the tenement flat in the middle of Glasgow in which we lived. For anyone in such an environment to have writing pretentions was treated with the utmost suspicion. More than that, it aroused in one's friends, neighbours and relations acute embarrassment, shame, discomfort and downright hostility.

A friend of mine, John Maloney, took this strange itch to write. He was a labourer of Irish descent and had no education worth mentioning. He belonged to a large, decent-living family on which nothing or no one had ever brought disgrace.

When John started shutting himself away in a bedroom not only to write but to address envelopes to himself and have what he'd written posted back to him, the family didn't know what to make of it. They held a family conference. Then one brother who was elected spokesman had a serious talk with John. All to no effect. Eventually the brother burst out in anguish and frustration.

"There's something far wrong with a man who writes letters to himself! If you'd just been a pouf the priest could have talked to you or one of us could have battered it out of you. But what the hell can anybody do about a writer?"

A writer was not only beyond the pale but beyond comprehension.

When I made what to me was the most earth-shattering, gloriously happy announcement of my life — of my first acceptance by a publisher — it so happened that some relations were visiting. I'll never forget their response after I'd breathlessly informed the family gathering of my success.

My announcement was met by total and utter silence. Eventually my mother, or someone, remarked on the weather and how wee Hughie's cold had gone from his chest. Then, in a great tide of relief from embarrassment, the conversation returned to familiar respectable lines.

I felt terribly ashamed. The unspoken belief had been confirmed, that there always had been something odd about me. I felt isolated too and that is why, when I eventually met other struggling working-class writers like John, I took them gratefully to my heart. I loved John as a brother and a dear friend, literally to the day he died.

When John received a cheque for the first story he had accepted, his mother became both frightened and distressed as if he'd perpetrated some sort of fraud or con-trick on the publisher. She ordered him to do the decent thing and send the money back. When John insisted he hadn't done anything dishonest she said there must have been a mistake then, so it was still the right thing to do to send it back.

He had a play accepted for television and the day the first review appeared his mother was shocked and said that theirs had always been a respectable family until then; never once had any of their names been in the paper.

My parents gradually came to terms with the problems of me being a writer although they never really accepted me as a *real* writer — not like authors they admired. My father never lived to see my first book accepted — something about which I've always been sad. But he was proud when he saw my first short story in print. He always shook his head though when I spoke of my ambition to be a novelist.

"I can't see how you can ever be a *real* writer when you haven't had a proper grounding in Shakespeare. If only you'd gone to the university like your mammy and I wanted you to."

(It's amazing how many people think that an academic education is essential to being a writer. I'll go into this in more detail in a later chapter.)

They had been so disappointed in me when I dug my heels in and refused to go to university. I wouldn't even have stayed on at school to sit my "O" Levels if I'd had my way but I was defeated by my mother in this. I had actually fixed up with a job in Grant's Bookshop in town. In celebration of what I thought was my first step into adulthood and the world of books I slept with my head covered in rag curlers and in the morning of the big day I combed my hair into a fashionably smooth "page-boy". (I'd always hated my curly Shirley Temple type hair.)

But when my mother heard that I was off to start work in Grant's Bookshop instead of going to school (I didn't have the nerve to tell her until the last moment), and when she saw my smooth hairstyle, she grabbed a brush and me, and battered and tugged the brush unmercifully over my head. She didn't stop until I was the most ghastly frizzy mess you've ever seen. My hair was literally standing on end all over. Then, despite my wails and broken-hearted sobbing and my red swollen face, she marched me into the centre of the city to Grant's Bookshop. There she demanded to see the manager and told him that I was not starting after all because I had to stay on at school and then go to university for a decent education.

Years later, after my books were published, my mother became aggressively loyal and insisted to everyone that I was a writer of tremendous talent, well-thought-of in the highest circles.

But in private she sighed and said she wished I could write nice books like Annie S. Swan.

# CHAPTER TWO

D.H. LAWRENCE showed an advance copy of his first book *The White Peacock* to his mother and later he said:

"She looked at the outside and then at the title page and then at me with darkening eyes. And though she loved me so much, I think she doubted whether it could be much of a book, since no one more important had written it. . . . It was put aside, and I never wanted to see it again. She never saw it again. . . ."

His father's reaction was typical and crushing.

"And what dun they gi'e thee for that, lad?"

"Fifty pounds, Father."

"Fifty pounds!" He was dumbfounded and looked at his son with shrewd eyes, as if he was a swindler. "Fifty pounds! An' tha's niver done a day's hard work in thy life!"

This is the next problem a tyro writer has to grapple with. No one he knows regards writing as work.

I remember I met a friend I hadn't seen for a while and she asked me what I was doing these days. When I replied, "I write books," she brushed this aside with, "Och, aye, but what do you *work* at?"

Often my mother burst out in harassment when she found me sitting in some corner with a notebook and pencil on my knee.

"There's a lot more important things you could be doing than sitting there scribbling. Give that floor a good scrub, for instance."

At night it infuriated my father the way I kept the light on till all hours. He was always reminding me that electricity cost money and to see me burning money away anyone would think I was determined that he should end his days in the poorhouse.

My father had the loan of a typewriter from the union when he was branch secretary and as soon as he found out I was using it he was so outraged he locked it away in the lobby cupboard. At the time I was young and selfishly obsessed with, as Maupassant said, "getting black on white", and I made no attempt to understand my father. I just seethed with resentment and hatred. I had no pretensions, at that early stage of being *A Writer*. I simply had this obsession about committing words to paper.

I realize now that my poor father was much tormented and hard put to it to guard his belongings from my mother. (She would even give things away at the drop of a hat. She once gave away to an old beggar woman a ring that had been given to me by my first boy-

6

friend and was of great sentimental value.) Having to contend with me as well was more than his flesh and blood could stand.

He was a big powerful man but an excruciatingly shy and private kind of person, except with children, of course. Left alone with children he became a child himself and flung himself into their make-believe world with great gusto. In a social adult environment, however, especially with my mother, he suffered agonies.

She was a slap-happy sociable woman of strong and stubborn will. She believed that when my father was behaving in any way differently from her he was just doing it for the hell of it, out of sheer wicked perverseness. She never let him get away with anything.

If she had visitors in the front room and my father insisted on hiding away in the living-room or bedroom she would purposely call out in a sing-song charming voice from the safety of the front room.

"Sa — a — am! Come on through and say hello to the ladies, dear."

Eventually, like a trapped animal, my father would appear to stand, anguished-eyed with one hand on the piano top as if for support. After clearing his throat several times he would say stiffly,

"Good evening, ladies. It's very nice to see you. I do hope you will have a pleasant and enjoyable evening."

The temptation to succumb to a polite round of applause was almost overwhelming and no one relaxed until he had disappeared again. Looking back, however, I can see that I had the fiction-writer's heightened awareness — what Dreiser called the "self-identification with every fault, frailty or futility". I knew how my father felt.

Much later, after everyone had gone, there would be a terrible row with my mother insisting that he had purposely acted like an idiot in order to make everyone, including her, feel awkward and embarrassed.

"You did that out of downright badness," she'd accuse.

Every effort to secure a private area of his life where he could be himself was scattered before the wind of my mother's cheerful carelessness.

His good hide-leather chair that he'd saved for for years and regarded, next to his books, as his most precious possession was violated by tea-cup rings on the arms and holes where needles and pins had been stuck in. Its velvet cushion was lumped out of shape with newspapers, magazines, combs, hairbrushes, biscuit crumbs, stockings and knickers being stuffed underneath.

He could never find his socks or his cuff-links although he'd put them carefully away in his drawer. The towel he insisted on having for his own was invariably found lying wetly where my mother had abandoned it. I've seen him go grey in the face and saucer-eyed with rage over my mother using his towel.

"You're mad," she used to say, "Away ye go and don't annoy me!"

His need to hang on to a bit of himself was as strong and as wild as my obsession for writing. I'm so sorry I was unable to cope with this in my teens. If I had been, I might have managed to avoid some bitter explosions between us. Like the time I decided to get up an hour or so earlier than I normally needed to, in order to get some writing done before leaving for work. I made the thoughtless error of taking my father's alarm clock (the only clock in the house) with the intention of resetting it and returning it to him in the morning.

Now, it was my father's pride that he had never been late for his work in his life and never taken a day off except when he had double pneumonia. For this obsessive conscientiousness he depended on the alarm clock. No one had ever been allowed to touch it.

He wound it every night with loving care and, believe it or not, in winter he used to wrap a woollen scarf round it because the cold seemed to adversely affect its workings. It affected our workings as well, as a matter of fact. That house was cold. If central heating had been invented we certainly had never heard of it and couldn't have afforded it if we had.

Anyway, my father got himself into a state of extreme agitation when he discovered his clock was not in its accustomed place. My explanations and assurances were to no avail. He loudly wanted his clock back. In a burst of frustration at the unfairness of life I threw the clock at him from the other end of the room. I can still see the horror on his face as he watched it bounce across the floor; the way his skin went a sickly grey and showed the stubble on his cheeks and chin, the way his dark eyes became anguished.

Tenderly he picked the clock up. He gazed at it, put his ear to it like an anxious doctor at a patient's chest. Then he wound it with meticulous care before wrapping it in a warm scarf and placing it beside his bed.

All this time my mother was telling him he'd drive anyone to throw things at him the way he behaved and that there were places for him in Hawkhead (the asylum) and he just tormented us all out of sheer badness. But later she came marching into my room and said,

"That was a terrible thing to do to your daddy. God was

8

watching you, you know, and He doesn't forget."

My father didn't say anything until next morning when he kissed me cheerio before going to his work.

"I'm sorry, hen," he said.

He was always the first one to apologize, indeed the only one if the altercation was between him and my mother. At least, my mother never apologized verbally in my hearing or to my knowledge.

I often wish I could have some of her supreme confidence in herself and in what she believed.

I remember early in my own marriage I had a quarrel with my husband and I made the mistake of pouring out my grievances to my mother. Her loyalty to me knew no bounds and she assured me that she would soon sort out that "devil" and that after she was finished telling him a thing or two the "wicked creature" wouldn't dare behave like that to me again.

Realizing my mistake I tried to calm the storm of indignation I'd raised.

"But, Mummy, there's two sides to every quarrel, you know."

"I know," she said. "You're right and he's wrong!"

It was the same principle she held to in her own mariage which, it seemed to me, was a continuous battleground. The only thing I can recall my mother and father ever agreeing on was that I should go to university.

My writing was never taken seriously enough for them to make an issue of it. It wasn't brought into any discussion of my future. If I was asked what I most wanted to do and I honestly said I wanted to write it was usually suffered with an indulgent,

"Aye, we know, hen, but what do you want to *work* at?"

I never mentioned the embarrassing subject of writing to anyone else, although I'd always *told* stories to my wee brother in bed every night. After my father's hair-raising tales which had left my young brother Audley and me clinging to each other in the dark in hysterical hilarity or fear or a mixture of both, a calmer, gentler tale was called for. My brother was a sensitive, highly-strung lad and I soothed him with fairy stories or stories about a wee boy like him and a wee girl like me and the wondrous good fortune that befell them. I made up the string of happy events as I went along. Our next-door neighbour's only child, Esther Kirby, used to sleep with us every time her mum and dad went out and she liked to hear my stories too. Every night both Esther and Audley would plead:

"Tell us a story, Margaret. Tell us a story."

During the day at school I told stories in the playground — serial stories that ended with a cliff-hanger at the sound of the bell

9

and was continued at the next playtime.

After school, especially during the dark winter evenings I dictated ghost stories and tales of horror to my girlfriend who was taking a secretarial course and needed practice with her shorthand. As a result I was so frightened by my imaginings I used to hare across the road from her to place to my own as if all the fiends of hell were after me. We lived in the top flat then and I took the stairs three at a time and nearly battered the door down in my anxiety to get into safety.

At the time of the Empire Exhibition an uncle and aunt came from some country area — I can't remember where — and took Audley and me to the exhibition with them for a treat.

Despite all my story telling — or maybe because of it — I was a timid and introverted child and when it came to sampling the thrills of the amusement park I hung back. I was a right spoil-sport and refused to set foot on even the slowest and most harmless-looking roundabout. My wee brother had a lot more courage and eventually, thoroughly sick of me and my "stupid carry-on", my aunt and uncle left me to my own devices and concentrated on sharing all the scream-raising amusements with Audley.

Next day at school my classmates were eager for news of my adventures. I didn't let them down. Never, I'm sure, had they heard of such a colourful and dangerous amusement park nor anyone who showed more courage in sampling its dangers than me.

I suppose that was just an extension of my stories to Audley and Esther. Sometimes, looking back, it seems that I quite often had stories thrust upon me, like the Christmas when Audley asked Santa for a Meccano set. Meccano sets were expensive. At least, they were to a family like ours. Recently a friend of mine was telling me how poor her family had been.

"Margaret," she said in hushed tones, "we even had frayed dinner napkins!"

I had to smile. I never even knew dinner napkins existed when I was young. Sometimes dinner didn't exist either.

My mother adored my wee brother and no wonder. He was such a lovable child with his chubby cheeks, large round eyes and breathless enthusiasms. There was never any hiding how Audley felt. He also had long thick lashes and a mop of curly hair which he said he hated because it was "sissy". He was an excitable and active child and he had the courage to fight against his many fears. This led him into lots of scrapes and adventures. But there were times when he could quietly become engrossed with plasticine. The stuff seemed to come to life in his hands and my mother took great

10

pride in showing off to friends models he made.

But this Christmas he asked not for plasticine but a Meccano set. I could see, even then, how my mother could not deny him it and I'm glad she didn't. He was always a bit delicate, despite his baby plumpness. Later in his teens he became gaunt and enormous-eyed from the pain he suffered with rheumatic fever. The heart condition it left him with killed him when he was still a young man.

The rheumatic fever was the result, I'm sure, of the damp bedroom he slept in. The wallpaper used to puff darkly off the walls and every night my mother used to try to dry his blankets and mattress in front of the living-room fire. I well remember the steam rising from them.

So when Audley asked Santa for the Meccano set my mother determined that by hook or by crook she was going to get him one. But her housekeeping had always been run on the "rob Peter to pay Paul" method and it must have taken quite a bit of financial juggling, desperate con-tricks, and sheer nerve to get the price of one out of her pittance of housekeeping money. She managed it. Unfortunately it meant she couldn't buy one other thing that Christmas — not even an orange for a stocking, and certainly not a present for me.

I remember how before Christmas she drew me aside and asked, "Would you like half a Meccano set for Christmas, Margaret?"

Knowing how Audley longed for one and sensing that it would please my mother if I said yes, I said yes. . . .

I loved my brother and accepted without any conscious thought and — as far as I can honestly remember — without any jealousy, that my mother loved him better than me. I never believed, in fact, that she loved me at all but I just accepted this as the normal order of things. I tried to please her though, on the off-chance that it might help. And it did please her when I said I wanted half a Meccano set for Christmas.

However, at the back of my mind I still believed that Santa would bring me a doll as well. But Christmas morning came and there on the rug in front of the living-room fire (usually a black smoky fire, I remember — "banked up with dross") sat one solitary box of Meccano.

Instinctively I knew that it was vitally important for me and my likeability rating to hide my true feelings. This I managed to do.

Then later that day when a neighbour asked me what I'd got for Christmas I told her in detailed and dramatic terms of how I had received a chocolate handbag and when I opened it there was a chocolate purse and when I opened that inside I found lots and lots of chocolate money.

I mention the incident of the "Meccano Christmas" not only because of the story I told about it but because it was a small yet important step in the development of the intuition, and the need to communicate that is necessary for a novelist.

And the first and most difficult thing to communicate, at least to family and friends, is the seriousness of your intention and the fact that writing is a real job of work.

# CHAPTER THREE

I COME BACK to the work aspect because it links in with beginner writers' lack of confidence, their lack of belief that they could become an author. One of the biggest stumbling blocks, if not the main hurdle to overcome is this sense of disbelief, of unreality, in yourself and others. Once you get over that then it's a matter of perseverance and learning to develop the characteristics and techniques that are needed to become a published writer.

Don't expect people's attitudes to change as soon as you get your first story published, however. When relations and friends hear that some editor or publisher has actually parted with good money for one of your stories the chances are they'll regard it as being the result of luck, not work.

In this context someone once said to Mark Twain that he was lucky and he replied: "Yes, and the harder I work the luckier I get!"

There's another attitude widely held and that is that anyone could write a marvellous book *if they had the time*. You've no idea how often a writer is told this. A novelist friend of mine had the plasterer in her house doing a job recently and he made the usual remark:

"I could write a marvellous book —" My friend waited for the infuriating bit; and it came — ". . . if I had the time!"

It does get annoying that and, as it happened, my friend felt a bit tetchy so she said:

"Well, even if I was given all the time in the world, I'd never be able to plaster a wall."

The plasterer answered: "No, I don't believe you could because you need a flair for it."

Well, all right, I accept that a plasterer needs flair. Does a novelist? What exactly does a novelist need?

Let me hammer this home once again before we go any further. Writing *is* work. It's *hard* work. Make no mistake about it. Don't believe these fairy tales you read in newspapers about writers dashing off a novel, getting it accepted right away and making vast fortunes overnight. It's maybe the first novel they have managed to get accepted. But that same novel has probably been rejected up to as many as seventy times before it found a home. (Yes, I've known of a writer who got her book accepted on her seventieth try.)

Lying about somewhere in a drawer or cupboard will also be —

on average — five previous novels that have been turned down by every publisher in London. There will no doubt be a history of many rejections in the short story field too as the writer has struggled to serve his or her apprenticeship and practise his or her trade.

As Irving Wallace said:

> Too many beginners seem to wish to be writers rather than to write. But there is no such thing as an Instant Author. A successful writing career usually takes years of hard solitary apprenticeship.

For years and years, sometimes for a lifetime, writers slog on without earning one penny. Or at best manage to scrape together a few hundred pounds a year to supplement another income earned by more regular methods in offices, shops, factories or shipyards. It's surprising how many people just take for granted that, having written your story, you'll automatically get paid for it. After all, in any other job or profession if you do a hard day's work, you get paid for it.

In this situation, I would say, to be a writer it takes guts, staying power, perseverance and not only an endless capacity but an absolute obsession for hard work. But, come to think of it, that's what most successful people have. I've met one or two self-made millionaires and they hardly ever stopped working. But their goal was money and power.

Don't get me wrong; a writer wants money too and I go along with Dr Johnson when he said, "No man but a blockhead ever wrote, except for money."

There are people who say they don't write for money and don't care if they never get published. They write for themselves, they say. Well, Victoria Holt, alias Jean Plaidy, gives these people short shrift. She said: "Those who don't write for money — can't!"

I used to feel very bitter at one stage, about not being able to get published. I looked at all the sugar-plum-fairy-tale-happy-ever-after stories about twinkly-eyed heroes and blonde blue-eyed heroines in women's magazines and I wept with frustration at how far removed from real life they were. And here was I only too well aware of the honest horrors of real life and nobody wanted to know. It was terribly galling. Especially when I needed the money. I burned with hatred at the unfairness and stupidity of editors and publishers. But not for long.

There comes a time when you've got to make a choice. Either you remain a self-pitying failure with a closed mind and a chip on your shoulder. Or, you take a deep breath, gird your loins, and try

14

to learn where you're going wrong in the presentation of what you honestly want to say. Then determine to continue serving your apprenticeship by practice, practice, practice until you can say it successfully as well as honestly and so reach your public.

Because a public you must have.

Irving Wallace said:

> A book, whether fact or fiction, must be honest above all, and after that it must communicate, grip, entrance someone else. Otherwise it has no reason to exist beyond feeding the author's self-indulgence and vanity. It takes not one but two people to make a book:
> The writer and the reader.

Maugham put it more succinctly: "A book is incomplete until it has a reader."

A novel should be an expression of your private, honest and unique self, honest but not undisciplined. Expression must be conveyed in narrative that will interest and entertain. If it is unprofessional and boring it will fail to be read and the author's higher purposes, if he or she has any, will never have a chance of being fulfilled. Part of being a professional is writing for money. But, of course, the professional writer doesn't write for money alone. This is proved by the fact that although he hopes to make it in the end, he seldom succeeds in acquiring any at the beginning of his career. Yet this doesn't stop him from "getting black on white".

Then, what does it take? It takes imagination and it helps as I've already suggested, if a writer's imagination was fired by being told stories in a highly stimulating and dramatic way in the formative years. Yes, a writer must have imagination, a very special kind of imagination and not only in dramatic intensity. It is tied up with another important part of a writer's equipment: an insatiable curiosity about people and what makes them tick. Imagination, the ability to find out how others live, or how they would want to live is, I believe, the basis of literature.

Henry James spoke of the writer's "power to guess the unseen from the seen, to trace the implications of things, to judge the whole piece by the pattern, the condition of feeling life in general so completely that you are well on your way to knowing any particular corner of it".

Wallace highlighted what is not only an important but fascinating aspect of the job: "My interest is in people and the hidden things in their lives. . . . My instinct is to take what's never shown on the surface and bring it to the surface. That's what makes a novel. . . ."

Dianne Doubtfire, author of the excellent book *The Craft of Novel-Writing*, says that there are characteristics which a large number of successful novelists have to some degree. The following is her list:

1) Unshockability.
2) Genuine interest in people (rather than things).
3) Not too much attention to material things.
4) Vivid imagination.
5) Observant eye.
6) Visual eye.
7) Childlike wonder and excitement about life.
8) Neurosis (abnormal sensitivity).
9) Curious eye on people in different settings and age groups etc.
10) Ability to overcome prejudices.
11) Extremist tendencies (fondness for exaggeration).
12) Many-faceted personality.
13) Doesn't mind, or can stand up to abuse.
14) Self-confidence (in writing self).
15) Got to care about tragedies of the world. Suffer with other people's sufferings.
16) Independence.
17) Lack of team spirit (must prefer to take all the blame or all the praise).
18) Honesty and sincerity.
19) No hypocrisy.
20) Willingness to admit faults.
21) Love of change and the unexpected.
22) Balance of sexes in one.
23) Perseverance.
24) Courage — guts.

John Braine who wrote another most helpful book, *Writing a Novel*, gives a shorter list. He says a writer needs:

1) Staying power.
2) A caring about people.
3) Habitual particularity of attention.
4) A mind that's lively and interesting in one way or another (not dull or limited).
5) An ability to cope with the problem of large-scale engineering in words.

I would go along with most of these things especially perseverance. And I would add intuition. My dictionary defines intuition as being the power of seeing the truth directly without reasoning. Intuition can be sharpened and developed with practice. Practice — that is another essential I would add to that list of what a writer should have. He needs practice in observation, practice in writing and practice in developing intuition.

Maugham said:

> . . . the great novelist needs a variety of parts, not only creativeness, but quickness of perception, an attentive eye, the power to profit by experience, and above all an absorbing interest in human nature.

A writer can appear slow-witted and absentminded yet can at the same time have the speed of light in picking up, seizing on to any tiny give-away sign or word or look or gesture. It's a selectivity of *significant* things. It's an alertness, an immediate and instinctive switching on to something that is in his line of business, the business of people and what makes them tick. It's something that comes with practice.

Maupassant said that great artists are those who impose their particular illusions on humanity and who see "the astonishingness of the most obvious thing".

This ties in with what Katherine Mansfield believed:

> . . . here are the inevitables — the realization that Art is absolutely self-development. The knowledge that genius is dormant in every soul — that that very individuality which is at the root of our being is what matters so poignantly.

Everyone who has ever wanted to write and had any secret dreams of becoming a writer should write down those words of Katherine Mansfield's, learn them off by heart, look at them and repeat them every day at least half-a-dozen times. *And believe them implicitly.*

I have met so many people who had a wonderfully rich vein of material in their lives to draw from. They even had the ability to recognize and tune into the significant, meaningful things they observed in people and events. They were interested in and cared about people. And they wanted to write. When I ask people like that why they don't write they invariably reply: "Oh, I'm not clever enough to be a writer." Or: "I haven't had a university education."

Neither had Stendhal.

Balzac was idle and troublesome at school and eventually went to work in an office. How he got on there is indicated by a note sent him one morning by the head clerk: "Monsieur Balzac is requested not to come to the office today as there is a lot of work."

Charles Dickens only had a few years' schooling as a young lad before being kept at home to help look after the other children in the family, clean the boots, brush the clothes and help the maid. In the intervals he just roamed about London.

Herman Melville, author of that strange and powerful book, *Moby Dick*, left school at the age of fifteen, worked as a clerk and eventually when he was seventeen he went to sea.

The school the Brontë sisters went to at Cowan Bridge was not only pretty useless but unhealthy. It killed two of them. Such schooling as Charlotte and Emily had after they were removed from Cowan Bridge seems to have been given them by an aunt.

At sixteen Dostoevsky went to school at the Military Engineering Academy and eventually got a job in the Engineering Department but left it because, as he said, "It was as dull as potatoes."

Tolstoy went to both the Universities of Kazan and Petersburg but was a poor student and took a degree at neither.

Sir Walter Scott remarked in his journal:

> What a life mine has been! — half-educated, almost wholly neglected or left to myself stuffing my head with most non-sensical trash and undervalued for a time by most of my companions. . . .

Robert Burns only managed to go to school in the little spare time he had from working on the farm.

At fourteen William Blake was apprenticed to an engraver.

At seventeen Kipling was working as a journalist.

Shakespeare left school when he was thirteen and was married by the early age of eighteen.

Gavarni said of Balzac that in general information on all subjects he had the crass ignorance of a moron. But when Balzac began to write, Gavarni continued, he had an intuition of things, so that he seemed to know everything about everything.

# CHAPTER FOUR

NO, YOU DON'T need an academic qualification to become a creative writer. You don't need a professorship, a PhD or an MA. You don't even need "A" or "O" Levels. These things, *while highly commendable and excellent in themselves* (many writers have academic qualifications, many do not) are irrelevant and immaterial as far as *creativity is concerned.*

It helps, as John Braine said, to have a lively and interesting mind as opposed to a dull one and most writers have at some time in their lives enjoyed reading a lot of books. But once you start writing you haven't much time for reading, unless it is research material that you need to read to help you with what you want to write. Maugham said: "I am not a scholar, a student or a critic, I am a professional writer and now I read only when it is useful to me, professionally."

Some people think it needs a particular kind of cleverness to write a historical novel and they have said to me: "I could never write a historical novel. I could never have learned as much as you did, for instance, to write your eighteenth-century books. I could never hold all that information in my mind."

Nor could I. I didn't need to. I know where to find the information when I want it. But more about that when I deal with research in another chapter.

The point I want to make just now is that the job of the academic, especially the lecturer in an English Department of a university and that of a creative writer are completely different.

So many people believe that because a man (or woman) works at a university, lecturing in English that it naturally follows he will also be able to *produce* what he talks about. Nothing is further from the truth. I stress this because for years I suffered from the delusion that academic knowledge about literature was the key to being able to write it. I regarded the academic's knowledge of literature and ability to be articulate about it with such awe and admiration that I was painfully inhibited by it, or, rather, by my lack of knowledge and lack of ability to be articulate in comparison.

The truth was brought home to me slowly, incredibly by meeting innumerable and brilliant academics who wanted to write, who *longed* to write, but simply couldn't do it. By "write" I mean create original fiction. The vast majority of them can put on paper theories or theses or works of criticism about creative writers but cannot become one themselves.

Long after I was a published writer and was making a decent income from my writing and my books were getting excellent reviews, I was still labouring under the delusion that if I went to extra-mural classes at the university and listened to the tutors there I would learn how to be a better writer. They, from their superior knowledge of literature, would be able to teach me. At first I found the classes interesting, then I became restless, then bored, then absolutely infuriated and near to exploding with impatience at the way the lecturer and the students endlessly analysed novels. Chapter by chapter, paragraph by paragraph, sentence by sentence was picked over and turned inside out and back to front in their efforts to find not one but a hundred and one different meanings. Each and every character was psychoanalysed. Innumerable guesses were made regarding what the characters would have done in other circumstances quite different from those of the story in which they belonged.

Eventually I couldn't help thinking: "What the hell am I doing here? Nobody, *especially* the tutor, knows a damned thing about writing. Not *how to do it!*"

I found myself becoming more interested in the tutor and the students as people. I sat watching them, their individual mannerisms and characteristics, and wondered what they were really like inside and what kind of lives they led. I listened to what they said and wondered *why* they said it. I suppose I was listening with a writer's ear and observing with a writer's eye but I didn't mean it to be obvious. The fact that it must have become uncomfortably so was brought home to me when a male student drew me aside one day as we were leaving.

"It might look as if there's something going on between me and Mrs Brown," he said, "but I can assure you our friendship is absolutely innocent!"

There was material for at least two dozen novels in that room and each person there was a character ready for the picking.

The most fascinating thing I learned by attending these classes, however, was the approach the tutors had to writing. I had and still have a great admiration for academics but I am now convinced that if you want to learn how to write creative fiction it is not to the academic you should turn for illumination. The only person who can help the beginner (apart from himself or herself) is a published creative writer.

Writers talking about writing are so *practical* in comparison.

I've been to many writers' schools and conferences and heard innumerable writers lecture and they really got down to brass tacks

20

and never mind the theorizing. The exception to this has been those writers who have been academics as well.

I have been in an audience of three hundred writers, a mixture of successful professionals and others at different stages of their apprenticeship, and the lecturer has turned out to be on sabbatical from some university. I have known a lecturer like this to reveal intellectual snobbishness and be subtly patronizing to the audience. Not that it mattered, because it made him interesting to observe as a person and I could just imagine three hundred minds beavering away as they secretly analysed him and wondered how they could use him in a story. But as his very literary thesis wound on its complicated way, the audience began to get restless. Some dozed off.

Other academics/writers kept you alert and interested by their sheer brilliance at composing and delivering a good lecture. It impressed and even entertained the audience. It gave them angles on how to be a successful speaker. It was seldom, however, much help to a struggling writer who wanted to know how to *write* successfully.

An academic who is also a writer is only of practical help when the writer part of him, the creative part, is strongest.

Creativeness is upset by analysis. If you attempt to write a story with parts of your mind pulling and worrying about whether you're doing it to the "proper rules" or if you're haunted by learned critics like Mr and Mrs Leavis breathing over your shoulder, the chances are your mind will block. You won't be able to write anything at all. At best it will spoil the sweep and faith in your story that is essential if you're going to write it. It will murder your courage in continuing and your pleasure in going on. Few writers are able to write against these handicaps.

I think this is what happens to academics who want to write but can't. And they are afraid of being held up to ridicule.

I have a friend who took two first-class honours degrees at Oxford. For years now she has been an excellent lecturer in the English Department of a university. She has always longed to write and recently she actually got down to it. I was delighted when I heard the news. This woman is a compassionate, caring person and she has such fascinating background material just begging to be used. Her life has been one seething mass of emotional conflict, idiosyncratic characters, suspense and drama. You name it, she's experienced it. She could be a female Tolstoy. But what is she trying to write? "A funny detective novel!"

Why a detective story? I wondered. Another lecturer of my acquaintance had told me just the week before that he was trying

21

to do the very same thing. And there had been others before that. It seemed odd to me. I supposed, however, that they must see it as an intellectual challenge. I knew that there was a great deal of inventiveness and technical expertise needed to write a detective novel and I always felt it too challenging, too difficult a genre to tackle myself.

Before I had time to ask my friend her reason for choosing this highly specialized type of writing, she said:

"I thought I'd try the detective novel because that way I wouldn't be setting myself too high a standard. No one could really make any sort of serious judgement against me then. I mean, I could always say, 'Well, it's only a detective story!'"

Then she kept repeating:

"I don't care if it isn't accepted, you know. It doesn't matter to me if it's rejected."

If she said that once, she said it at least a dozen times within a couple of hours. I was forced in the end to conclude that it mattered to her far too much.

My other friend, the one I mentioned who told just me the week before that he was writing a detective novel, went as far as reading me the first chapter. He was a good, confident reader. He also had writing talent and I told him that the part of the chapter in which he dealt with the school situation was excellent. It really came to life and had a ring of authenticity. You felt he really knew what he was talking about in the school scenes and he could convey them vividly and entertainingly. Where he'd gone wrong, I ventured to point out, was in the other part when he'd got rather carried away in a philosophical argument about conservation. If he cut that out. . . .

I had softened my criticism of course by stressing that it was only my opinion (something I suspected he wouldn't be likely to think much of). And I refrained from quoting Hardy who said that a novel is an impression not an argument.

Unfortunately, it turned out that the school scenes were just a one-off by-the-way job in the first chapter. The conservation question was to be the nucleus of the whole book. Apparently he was planning to elevate the lowly detective novel on to a higher plane. But in Joyce Cary's words: "I don't care for philosophers in books. They are always bores. A novel should be an experience and convey an emotional truth rather than an argument."

I think my friends have the wrong approach to writing and especially to writing the detective novel. I can't see either of their books reaching publication standards. But I hope I'm wrong.

I suspect that part of their trouble is that it's not so much that they want to write — they want to be writers. There's a difference.

But alas, as Malcolm Cowley said in one of the Hopwood Lectures: "The sort of training that is best for a future critic or teacher — the sort given in our best univesities — is often dangerous to an apprentice writer. If he spends too much time on the close analysis of texts, the critical side of him ceases to be a listener, making its critical comments in an undertone; the voice of the critic becomes louder, firmer, more admonitory, and perhaps the other voice, that of instinct or emotion, may be frightened back into the depths of the mind."

Writing, I repeat, is a different ball-game altogether.

To quote Somerset Maugham:

> The Creators produce because of that urge within them that forces them to exteriorize their personality. It is an accident if what they produce has beauty; that is seldom their special aim. Their aim is to disembarrass their souls of the burdens that oppress them, and they use the means, their pen, their paints, their clay, for which they have by nature a facility.
>
> Artistic creation is a specific activity that is satisfied by its own exercise. The work created may be good art or bad art. This is a matter for the layman to decide. He forms his decision from the aesthetic value of the communication that is offered to him. If it yields escape from the reality of the world he will welcome it, but is very likely at best to describe it only as minor art; if it enriches his soul and enlarges his personality he will rightly describe it as great. But this I insist, has nothing to do with the artist. . . . He has already had his reward in the satisfaction of his creative instinct.

I agree.

The writer certainly crosses out and scores and makes corrections while he's writing. He'll make changes as better ideas for characters or scenes occur to him.

What he's aiming at is to make the printed page disappear, to draw the reader away from the surface of the page he is reading to join, in the world of his imagination, the character he is reading about.

In his efforts to achieve this aim the writer will rewrite the whole thing, and perhaps again and again and again. But this is all part of the creative process. And while this process is going on nobody should be further from the writer's thoughts than critics, no matter how knowledgeable, highly intelligent or articulate they might be.

# CHAPTER FIVE

WHEN SOMEONE said to Harold Robbins that his life sounded like a Harold Robbins novel he replied: "What do you mean it sounds like a Harold Robbins novel? It is a Harold Robbins novel and I've been writing it for thirty years!"

The stuff of a man's writing is the stuff of his life. But even if you realize this when you are at the beginning of your writing career it's no use sitting down one day with a blank sheet of paper in front of you and racking your brains trying to think of something to write about. That's not the way to go about it at all. When I was beginning I didn't realize this. I didn't know then that writing was about *feeling*.

Tolstoy made this point over and over again:

> Art is a human activity consisting of this, that one man consciously by means of external signs, hands on to others, feelings he has lived through, so that others are infected by these feelings and also experience them.

To be able to write, he maintained, one had to "evoke in oneself a sensation which one has experienced before, and having evoked it in oneself, to communicate this sensation in such a way that others may experience the same sensation. . . . So that other men are infected by these sensations and pass through them; in this does the activity of art consist."

On another occasion he said: "Real art depends first on feeling. . . He (the author) should be driven by an inward need to express his individual feeling. . . ."

First, then, an author has to have feelings, good or bad. And the stronger the better. In fact, better still, a writer should write from something that obsesses him. Apart from anything else, this gives the drive, the desperate energy needed to complete book after book.

There's also got to be an obsession for writing, for the actual putting of words down on paper. Lots of writers I know, including myself, even have an affection for the paper and all the accoutrements of writing. I really enjoy looking in a stationer's window or wandering about inside the shop. The sight of all that virgin paper, all those lovely notebooks and pens and pencils and rubber bands fill me with pleasure and satisfaction, even happiness. This is something else one's non-writer friends don't understand. I knew exactly how John Maloney felt when he said to me:

"I wish to God my family and friends would stop giving me presents of socks and soap and bloody after-shave at Christmas, Margaret. If only they'd give me something useful, something I'd really appreciate — like a ream of typing paper!"

I knew at the beginning that I had the obsession for putting words down on paper. I was not aware at the time, however, of the deeper obsessive feelings I suffered from and still suffer from.

I started to write little descriptions of things that caught my attention; a tree, a sunset, the moon, clouds. Clever-sounding phrases that occurred to me were recorded in my notebook. Brief pen-sketches of people that I met or noticed in the street were conscientiously included. I also kept a diary.

As far as I can remember I have never used anything from these notebooks or diaries. I don't regret them though. I was developing a love of words. I was practising writing words down. But, most important of all, I was developing observation, intuition and selectivity. These things at that far-off time were weak and under-nourished but they were there. I was using my eyes. I was interested in people and things around me. Something, I didn't know what, made me pick out certain people and certain things. The observation of *significant* things is vitally important. It ties up with *selectivity*.

Now, I believe that there is creativity in everyone and it can be channelled into all sorts of pursuits like sewing and knitting and cooking and carpentry and sculpture and painting and writing etc.. Whatever creative thing you feel you want to do, if you work hard enough at it and learn enough about it you'll do it and do it successfully. The only thing that worries me about some people's writing potential is the selectivity aspect. I'm not so sure that this is something that can be learned. But I may be wrong. I'm only saying this because in the many years I have now spent in helping beginner writers in workshops and tutorials and the like, it is the one thing that I've noticed some people find great difficulty in understanding.

Let me give you an example.

Years ago I was asked by a writers' club to adjudicate a serial story competition. The entries were submitted anonymously. One particular story immediately gripped my attention and interest. It was written by somebody who obviously knew something about history or had done a good job on research. It showed a vivid imagination too. Here, I thought, must be the competition winner. But as I read on I became more and more confused and disappointed. The original story-line had splintered off into this direction and that direction. And the splinters had splintered —

this way and that way until it was just a complicated meaningless jumble.

I awarded the prize to someone else but I asked who the author of the historical piece was because I wanted to have a chat with her. It turned out to be a librarian who had indeed a splendid knowledge of historical fact. I tried to explain to her that she had far too much irrelevant fact in her serial story. I told her that she'd started with an excellent idea and if only she had stuck to this. . . .

She interrupted me indignantly to insist that everything in her serial had been essential information. But, Moravia pointed out: "If we do not wish to select then even 10,000 words would not be enough to describe a room."

Years later that woman was still unpublished, still writing book length stories, and still making the same mistake. It's tragic because she has such a good imagination, such good material, and she's not afraid of working hard. I do wish I could have helped her and I did try on many occasions over the years. Perhaps someone else will succeed where I failed.

This same librarian assisted me on one occasion with research. I asked if she'd check over the typescript of my first historical novel, *The Prince and The Tobacco Lords*. I had already checked and double checked the book myself and felt confident I hadn't made any mistakes but I always treble check if I get the chance. I thought that if there was any small error in the food or costume of the period this was the woman to spot it.

In the brief prologue of this book, Sheriden, Prince Charles's tutor, is thinking of what a couple of people have said about the prince's planned invasion of England. One of the people happened to be somebody called Earl Marischal. The quote in Sheriden's thoughts amounts to a couple of short sentences and its only significance is the attitude to the invasion. Even the invasion and the prince himself is only significant in the book as far as they affect the main characters of the story which are really the Tobacco Lords of Glasgow and their families.

But the mistake I had made, according to my librarian friend, was in failing to tell who Earl Marischal was and where he'd come from and where he lived and who his father was and what his background had been. She told me in detail the history of Earl Marischal's house and all the people who'd previously lived there and their histories. Other names associated with these people cropped up and she gave me their histories too until I became lost in a maze that became more and more complicated and further and further away even from Earl Marischal. (Not to mention my story of Adam Ramsay and his daughter Annabella and their

26

washerwoman's children Regina and Gav.)

I thought it illustrated perfectly how she went wrong in her own writing.

My point is, a writer has got to be selective. It's more important to know what to leave out than what to put in. I suppose it's a kind of instinct. So much in this writing business is intuitive. I know I'm on difficult ground here. Trying to explain what this instinct is and how to develop and sharpen it is like trying to grasp shadows or mountain mist and pin them under a microscope. I think the best way to illustrate what I mean is by revealing wisps of my own experience.

My earliest instinctual memory was a vague feeling of being in a cot. Through the darkness of time I caught glimpses of wooden cot bars. I concentrated my attention on this experience, this feeling of being in a cot. Soon I became aware of being near an old-fashioned black grate with a gas mantle above it to its right side. I didn't have a clear picture of this in my mind's eye. Yet the more I concentrated — not so much my mind but my *senses* on the scene — I *knew* that the cot was in a small room in front of a fireplace and close at the side of a high set-in-the-wall bed. On that bed lay the humped figure of my mother. I had not so much the sight — everything was dark and shadowy and incomplete — but the *impression* of these things.

I didn't feel any pain or remember any sound but I knew I was crying. Then I had the sensation of a man bending over the cot, lifting me out and dressing me in a tiny velvet dress. It was dark red in colour. My memory wasn't in colour. Everything was still in shadow. I just felt that it was dark red in the same way that I knew the man was my father.

Now comes what to me is the most interesting and significant bit. I felt, coming from the bed in which my mother lay, a wave of absolute hatred. More than hatred. It was repulsion. It was that emotion emanating from my mother that returned to me most clearly and vividly remained with me ever since.

That feeling that my mother hated and rejected me affected my whole life more than I can say. And it's only recently — sadly long after my mother's death — that two things occurred to me. One, my mother might have been pregnant with my wee brother at the time and feeling unwell and not able to get up and attend to me herself. And, two, if I was screaming and screaming and she felt ill and unable to cope and just longed for a bit of peace and quiet, wasn't it natural that the poor soul would — even just for that night or that moment — hate me? She could have loved me again the next minute or the next day but I just haven't remembered that.

27

I often ask myself, if I had not received that terrible emotional barrage from my mother that awakened my instinct, that alerted my intuition, would I ever have become a novelist? I'm perfectly serious about this. Just as my father vividly stimulated my imagination, so my mother brought to intense life my instincts and emotions.

I maintain that these things are important in the making of a novelist.

When I wrote my published novels I was simply telling stories according to the technique I'd learned over the years with all my practice in writing. I was surprised when a friend remarked to me one day.

"Do you realize that your books have a common theme running through all of them?"

"What theme?" I asked.

"Rejection."

On checking over my books I had to admit that — yes — in *The Breadmakers*, Catriona's mother literally hated her guts and Melvin the man she married is still in love with his first wife. In *A Baby Might Be Crying* Madge's husband has affairs with other women. In *A Sort of Peace*, Julie's mother-in-law hates and rejects her. In *The Prisoner*, Celia's husband prefers his homosexual lover. In the eighteenth-century trilogy Regina is abandoned by her mother and rejected by her husband. In my nineteenth-century book *The Dark Side of Pleasure*, Augusta's mother has her thrown out of the house. Luther, the hero (?), is forced to marry her and takes her to his bosom with as much love as he would a millstone or a praying mantis.

Well, maybe my friend is right but there's a lot more to my books than that. There is I hope first and foremost, what one tutor wrote in red ink on an essay I had attempted on the subject he'd given which was the Poor Law of 1834. He wrote alongside my fail mark: "A cracking good tale!"

I doubt if I will ever write a good essay but I hope I'll always be able to tell a good story that will interest and entertain as well and help people to understand each other better.

To do this you've certainly got to try to understand yourself. It helps to take an interest in and to read something about psychology. I don't mean to struggle through technical tomes. But there are lots of easily digested books for the layman on the market. I have had wonderful help both as a writer and a person by reading a book called *Psycho-Cybernetics* by Maxwell Maltz. Don't be put off by the title. It's a perfectly simple, easy to understand book. And I remember a fascinating extra-mural course I once took on "The

Study of the Personality". The lecturer, a young psychiatrist, was really excellent and illustrated everything in human terms from his casebook of patients he'd treated. I never actually used in my stories any of the case histories he told us about. Nevertheless he helped develop and deepen my understanding of myself and my fellow human beings in a way that was of great practical use to me in my writing.

You see, writing isn't finding or deciding on a subject to write about. Writing is *being*.

Pearl Buck said:

> Writing novels absorbs the entire life and being. If the sacrifice of life and being is not joyfully made, then it should not be made at all.

# CHAPTER SIX

DYLAN THOMAS said he wrote poems as stepping stones out of his own darkness. I think this indicates not only the quest for understanding that I have been talking about but a cathartic element in a man's or woman's writing. It is Maugham's "disembarrassment of the soul". Although, of course, as I've previously suggested, a writer may not be conscious of this while working on a novel. Yet while he is working on a novel a writer must be supremely and courageously himself or herself. That way you develop your own style.

Style is the total of you as a writer. It is made up of knowledge, experience, technique, a love of words, and your own personality. I believe it is the personality part which matters most, and the more complex and multifarious the characteristics contained in it the better. After all, if you're going to write about lots of characters — men, women and children of different types, you've got to be able to get under the skin of lots of different types.

To do this you've got to sharpen your sensibilities. You've got to practise self-identification with your material. You've got to see it, as it were, as intimate and as *warm* as yourself. You've got to observe people, especially the significant, meaningful, give-away things about them. For instance, as well as the smiles and loving words of the married couple giving the party at which you're a guest, you must be quick enough to notice that one glance flashing between them which betrays secret resentment and conflict.

In the middle of a mother's proud and happy talk about her perfect son, you must detect that tiny sigh and moment of vagueness in the eyes that gives away the truth.

You can't do this if you're continuously chattering and enjoying centre stage yourself. There are times of course when writers do this, and I'm no exception. But not all the time. Most times, except perhaps among close friends with whom I can relax and let myself go, I'm a background person. I leave others to enjoy the limelight and do the talking. That way I'm free to listen and watch, to closely observe people. But I'm tuning in to them as much if not more with my "emotional antennae" than with my ears and eyes. From that first intuitive experience as a baby this antennae has developed, with much concentration over the years. It has flourished in rich soil.

As I mentioned earlier, my brother was a delicate lad and my mother, quite understandably, lavished much more time, attention and love on him than she did on me. I didn't understand at the time. She was always leaving my father and sometimes she'd take both Audley and me with her. More often than not, however, she would not take me. (Sometimes I ended up away somewhere on my own.) As a result when I set off for school each morning I could never be sure if she and my brother would be there when I returned or what was going to happen to me. To a child of primary-school age this is, to say the least, an insecure lifestyle. Every morning before I set off for school I used to kiss my mother, then gaze up at her, desperately trying to tune into her, to sense if she was going to leave me. Every single day after I went out and shut the door I couldn't force myself to walk away from it. I had this compulsion to knock and bring her back to me so that I could kiss her once again.

She used to get so irritated with me I'm sure she could have cheerfully strangled me. I felt the irritation straining out even though she struggled valiantly to control it. Only once did she ever strike me and I haven't the slightest recollection of the actual blow. All I remember is that one day she called me over to her knee and apologized for "raising her hand".

All day and every day at school what the teacher said or did, what the other children said or did only skimmed vaguely over the surface of my attention. It reminds me of what Harold Robbins once said when talking of how he felt while writing a novel:

"I'm right here, and yet I'm not right here. I'm doing everyday things I have to do and yet my head is somewhere else. And I never really come together."

I just existed, hung in suspense from the moment I left the house until I returned there again. Tension would mount as I approached the road, then the building, and by the time I entered the close and reached the doorstep I was on the point of secret collapse. I knocked at the door and waited, my whole being centred on listening for my mother's jaunty stride along the lobby, willing it to come.

If I peered through the letterbox and saw newspapers spread over the linoleum and smelled disinfectant, I knew she had gone.

Normally my mother had a cheerful disregard for housework. But when she left my father she always did so in a burst of cleaning and scrubbing as if literally washing her hands of him forever.

I would stand for a while on the doormat before going to sit on the stone steps of the close. I wasn't trying to remember what shift my father was on and when he'd be home. I wasn't wondering if my mother would be away for a day or a week or a month. She'd gone and I was in a state of shock.

Looking back, this kind of experience has been invaluable to me because it wonderfully concentrated my sensitivities. For one thing I know how a child can feel. I know that ideas of time, the past, the future, mean nothing. There is no future.

Eventually neighbours would see me and take me in. They were kind but I sensed what a nuisance I was hanging about, albeit quietly, while they were busy making their tea. As soon as I saw from the window my father coming along the street, I would make my way slowly downstairs. My father was a man of uncertain temper and the discovery of the loss of my mother was always a terrible thing to behold. What's more, to be lumbered yet again with me was an extra punishment he needed like a hole in the head.

There is a rich enough bank of emotion to draw from in that particular experience to supply my needs for several, indeed endless, novels. Not that one lifts experience straight from life. That would be reportage. A creative artist doesn't copy life. He makes an arrangement of it to suit his own purpose. He's not concerned about whether it's a truthful likeness of the original characters or incidents. This would be inhibiting. The fiction-writer wants to create a plausible harmony convenient to his story. For that he's got to be selective.

Alfred Hitchcock said that drama is real life with the dull bits cut out. One certainly has to keep this in mind when writing a novel.

But what one must put over honestly and accurately is the original feeling. The feeling need not necessarily spring from an incident in your own life although it will probably be coloured by your own emotional experience. Novels are basically about people and stories and story characters come into being by the writer observing and becoming moved or excited by facets of real-life people. His imagination is excited and he is emotionally moved. As a result he feels compelled to communicate this excitement, this emotion to his readers. *What the writer has felt at the beginning, the reader must feel at the end.*

That is a very important thing for the beginner writer to remember. I wish someone had told me this when I was writing my first novel. I just set to, not knowing anything. I produced an autobiographical, undisciplined (and, I suspect, self-pitying) splurge; a kind of shapeless outpouring. It must have been about the size of *Gone With The Wind* and it took a lot of tearing up and burning. This is what I evidently did with it. You see, all it conveyed to me on reading it was disgust and embarrassment, and that was not what I, as a writer, had intended to convey. Therefore it was a failure. I knew it instinctively.

With my next book, at least I made an attempt to tell a story. This was about wealthy people who lived in a country mansion filled with priceless antiques. At that point in my life I had never met any wealthy people nor had I seen the inside of a country mansion. It might not have been so bad if I'd known how to do research but I'd never heard of research. I just conjured it all up out of my imagination.

Still, I was learning certain techniques with practice. By the time I was on my third book I was getting the hang of dialogue. I was reading it out loud to check for clumsy sounding or too "literary" talk. It was beginning to occur to me that dialogue was a distillation, a concentration of speech, and that it had four main purposes:

1) To show character.
2) To further the action of the plot.
3) To convey needed information.
4) To show the emotional state of the speaker.

I was noticing that in ordinary conversation people were always butting in to each other, that people communicated fitfully and never quite in time.

I was becoming less afraid of using "he said" and beginning to realize that it was amateurish to be always struggling for alternatives. I was learning simple rules of presentation such as: new speech, new line. But if the action connected with the speaker interrupts his dialogue then the rest of the dialogue can continue on the same line.

Presentation is important and can be a terrible worry to beginners and a subject about which they are often too embarrassed or ashamed to admit ignorance.

I have taken a meeting of beginner writers that has sat in silent awe on previous occasions listening to lecturers talk to them about commitment or symbolism. All they were longing to know was what size of paper you're supposed to use and whether to type in single or double spacing and what to do with the damned thing once you've got it typed.

Nowadays, by the way, A4 paper is the thing, thick for the top and thin for the copy and always take at least one carbon copy of everything you type. Double spacing is a must and be sure to leave a decent-sized margin at the left-hand side and a good space at the bottom of every page. There's a reason for this. Printers, and often people in the publisher's office too (once the book's accepted) need to make notes in the margin. I've been told that the space at the bottom is needed because of the way the pages are clipped on to a machine at the printers.

I used to fasten each of my chapters separately with a paper clip, put them all into a cardboard envelope-type folder, secure it with an elastic band and then put that into a large padded envelope. Or alternatively I wrapped the folder in brown paper and tied it up with string.

Now I like to punch a couple of holes through the left side of all the pages and lace them *loosely* together with a tag. The point is you don't want to prejudice publishers' readers against your work by having something that is so tightly fastened together they can hardly open it and when they do daren't let go or it immediately springs shut. It's more convenient if the pages can lie flat and remain flat. Never condemn the reader to wrestle with fiendishly strong spring clips in binders that are like a sack of coal to lift up and down.

Do remember that the publisher's reader is only human. A good idea is to read a book called *Reader's Report* by Christopher Derrick. I heartily recommend it. It tells you all the reasons why readers give the thumbs down on a book — what impresses them and what distresses them.

One publisher told me that he prefers his writers to place all the pages of their manuscript (without any fastening) into an old typing-paper box, the kind with a lid that normally holds a ream of paper, put a large rubber band round the box then parcel it up with brown paper and string.

As for where to send it — you should browse around libraries and bookshops to find out what publishers are publishing what kind of books and send your novel to the publisher that seems to be doing your type of story.

Before you do anything however, you should buy yourself a copy of *The Writers' and Artists' Year Book*. Every writer must have one. Inside you'll get the names and addresses of all the publishers and the subjects they deal in and much else.

And of course when you do post your novel always, always remember to enclose a note and a postal order or stamps to cover return postage. it's enough that the note (typewritten of course) should say:

Dear Editor,

I enclose my novel called ——— . I hope that you will like it and find it suitable for your list.

I also enclose a postal order to cover return postage should this be necessary.

Yours sincerely,

...............................................

Keep a carbon copy of all letters. A record book is also necessary. It need only be a school jotter but it must list the title of the book sent, when it was posted and to whom. Other two columns should be reserved for when it was accepted or returned.

After you have posted your MS to the publisher, forget about it and get cracking with another novel. You'll save yourself a lot of agonizing suspense that way and a lot of listening and watching for postmen.

Publishers are incredibly cruel, thoughtless and uncaring monsters. Or so they seem to beginner writers.

They should send an acknowledgement of delivery within a week or ten days but they seldom do. They should give a decision four or five weeks after the acknowledgement as to whether or not they intend publishing your book. (I once attended a public meeting where a publisher said that there was no reason why any publisher should take longer than one month to come up with a "Yes" or "No".) They almost never do. I've known an author to sweat it out for two years before getting a decision. The general public just don't know the slings and arrows of outrageous fortune that a struggling writer has to suffer.

Of course, I must be fair and point out that publishers have a lot to suffer from writers as well. Publishers, in fact, can be extremely charming and kind. I have always had a good, friendly relationship with my publisher and I'll never forget, on my first visit to London for the publication of *The Breadmakers* how I got lost on the way and arrived later than expected. I telephoned my publisher and, would you believe it, at about one in the morning he came and rescued me from Trafalgar Square and deposited me safely in the hotel where he'd earlier booked a room for me. I can still see in my mind's eye, the lovely arrangement of flowers in that room and I later discovered that his wife had been responsible for this thoughtful and welcoming touch. On another occasion I was in London whooping it up with a girlfriend having a rare old time going to theatres, exhibitions etc. I spent all my cash and in my innocence I offered a cheque in payment for my hotel bill at the end of the week without a banker's card. No one had ever bothered to ask me for a banker's card in Glasgow. I was forgetting of course that London is a bigger place and I'm not quite so well known there! The hotel couldn't even telephone my bank to see if my credit was good because by this time the banks were shut. They refused to accept my cheque and in acute distress, embarrassment and panic I 'phoned my publisher who immediately dispatched a colleague from his office to settle my bill.

That's how publishers *can* be.

But to get back to you, as a beginner. After about six weeks you should write a polite note of enquiry.

But then what? The trouble is, you see, that the beginner is terrified to rock the boat. You're desperate to get your book, your baby, the child of your mind and heart and soul accepted. You worry about rubbing the publisher the wrong way by pestering him with yet another letter of enquiry. What if he had been meaning to accept the book but this particular day he happened to be suffering from a hangover and just had to get his spite out on somebody? Along comes your letter and brings you to his misery-laden head-throbbing attention and he turns to his secretary and says,

"Send her book back, for God's sake, and get her out of my hair!"

You can't bear it. You write every variation of letter from sharp indignant ones to pathetic pleading ones. *Nothing makes one whit of difference.*

I must warn you that although writing is a joy despite all the hard work, once you step into the market place of publishing, it can be absolute hell!

# CHAPTER SEVEN

THIS BRINGS me yet again to the personality aspect. This is one of the reasons why I say that perseverance is a must for anyone who hopes to become a writer. Many talented people fall by the wayside after receiving even just one rejection slip. But it's when you get a hundred and one that you begin to worry.

It was years before it even occurred to me that anyone might actually want to buy my scribbles. After that it took quite a long while to save up to have what I'd written, typed. Then there was all the time trying to find out where to send it. But I still persevered with writing whenever and wherever I got the chance.

At one time I was working in a shoe shop that shut for lunch. So I took sandwiches and determined that after the boss went home for her lunch I'd get out my novel and do a bit of work on it. I discovered, however, that once the doors were shut and the shop went quiet, an army of mice appeared. Nothing daunted, I took my piles of paper and a chair and sat in the doorway. This meant I was in full view of the street and causing quite a stir of interest among passers-by. I managed to ignore these distractions. I couldn't ignore the boss's fury, however, when she returned to find people's attention more on a mess of papers in her doorway than the shoes in her window.

I was visiting a friend the other week and she was chatting about old times and one thing she recalled that I'd forgotten.

"I could never understand you when we were young, Margaret."

"How's that?" I asked.

"Well, so often I'd say, 'Come on, let's go to the dancing tonight,' and you'd say, 'I can't; I've got to stay in and write.'"

Although of course I did get to the dancing sometimes and I met a young man and got married and had a baby.

By the time my son was about three I was dragging him along the street to the nearest day nursery so that I could organize a few hours of writing. I really mean dragging, because the poor wee soul didn't want to go and screamed loudly and brokenheartedly. I feel distressed and guilty about doing this to him even now. In fact, quite recently I was feeling over-sensitive and this began to prey on my mind until I couldn't stand it any longer. I burst out to Kenneth (who is now a strapping six feet and a brown belt in karate):

"I'm sorry for forcing you to go to that nursery, son. I've always regretted it, I knew I shouldn't have done it when it upset you so much."

He rolled his eyes. "For goodness sake, Mum! I've forgotten all about that years ago."

But I didn't feel any better until he'd given me one of his comforting bear hugs.

My third novel, even looking back now, wasn't too bad. As I said, at least I was beginning to get the hang of technique. I was acquiring self-discipline in the actual handling and ᵗting down of my material. I was learning how to be ruthless. ᵼ was spotting repetitions and slashing them out. It was beginning to occur to me that when I was anxious to put over some point or create some emotional response, I didn't succeed half so well if, in my anxiety to show how important it was, I went on and on about it (or had one of my characters go on and on about it).

It's strange but true that the more you pare down the words you use on these occasions (making sure of course that the words left are exactly the right words to convey your meaning precisely) the more punch the scene is likely to have. Characters spring to life more vividly too, emotion is more effectively aroused and your point gets straight home if your prose is not too long-winded, over-explanatory, repetitive, or cluttered with adjectives.

This is something a beginner novelist simply must learn. It has often surprised me how even writers who have succeeded in other fields make the mistake of over-writing when they come to tackle their first novel. I remember a man who had spent a lifetime as a successful journalist showing me a book he had written. For years this book had been bouncing backwards and forwards from practically every publisher in the land. Eventually he had accepted defeat and given up.

I asked to see the manuscript and after reading it it was quite obvious to me that he had a perfectly good, publishable story — once all the dead wood that was hiding it had been ruthlessly cut away. With his permission I slashed my pencil through page after page of it. The result was that when he tried the book out again he got it accepted. He's now happily working on his second novel which is a cracker. He's not going to make the same mistake again.

Lots of people do, though — again and again and again.

There are various reasons for this. One is that some people find it difficult to accept and act on criticism. I'm not saying that you should just accept as gospel every word everyone says about your manuscript and obediently and unquestioningly act on their advice. There are times when you should stick to your guns and to hell with everyone.

Maugham said of critics:

> The critic who is not himself a creator is likely to know little
> about the technique of the novel and so in his criticism he
> gives you his personal impressions — which may be of no
> great value. Or he proffers a judgement founded on hard and
> fast rules which must be followed to gain his approbation. As
> if a shoemaker made shoes in only two sizes and if neither
> fitted your foot you could for all he cared go shoeless.

All the same, as far as criticism is concerned I believe it does no
harm to cultivate a patient ear, a thick skin and an open mind.

I have found that giving my typescript to two, perhaps even
three friends to read before I send it off to the publisher can be
most helpful. I get their reactions as ordinary readers. The danger
here is that because they are friends they may be too kind in their
comments. Sometimes it's the other way around. They have liked
the book and have really nothing bad to say about it but, forced
into what they feel is the role of critic, they believe they are duty
bound to say something. So they pounce on punctuation or just
carp about anything at all.

Or sometimes they truly hate the story and give it to you straight
from the shoulder with what seems to you at the time to be fiendishly malicious glee. Again, this is where self-discipline comes in
very handy. There's no use attacking your friend in retaliation.
After all, you asked for it! It's also a waste of time to hotly defend
your masterpiece. Although, especially at the beginning of our
careers, most of us do.

The best way is to listen patiently and swallow your irritation
and the painful lump in your throat. Thank your friends for their
honest opinion. Tell them that you'll think it over. Tell them that
when you re-read the book yourself you'll keep in mind what
they've said. And do just that. Give yourself a couple of days to
cool down and recover. Then read your typescript again and ask
yourself if there could be anything at all in your friends' criticism
or suggestions that might improve the telling of *what you want to say*.

Often your friends won't know what's wrong with the book.
Something, some part of it has jarred on them, has bored them, has
"turned them off". They think they know exactly how and why
you've gone wrong and as often as not they think they know how
you should put it right. This is seldom true. But their reactions are,
nevertheless, very valuable. The mere fact that a certain part of the
book has jarred on them in any way is significant. And if that same
part has the same or similar reaction on two or three friends who
have had no contact with each other, then this ought to indicate

that this particular part of your book needs more of your serious consideration and attention.

It might just be that, as I've already indicated, you've been pressing your point too hard or too long. Or you've botched the writing in some other way and just not succeeded in conveying the picture you had in your mind to the reader.

I remember, a lifetime ago, sending a story to a D.C. Thomson magazine. I got it back with the following letter:

> Thank you for letting us see your story "Flashpoint" which I am now returning to you.
>
> You write very fluently but one essential point to bear in mind when writing for popular women's magazines is that your main character must be likeable. Misguided, deluded or slow in the uptake are all permissible provided she is likeable with it. I felt what Nancy needed was a punch in the mouth!
>
> Perhaps the easiest way to avoid this trap is to model your character on somebody you like who has a similar problem, then you can't go wrong.
>
> I hope we'll be seeing some more stories from you soon.

That hurt at the time. I had thought Nancy *was* likeable. But after I recovered my equilibrium I read the story again. I discovered, to my surprise, that the Nancy on my typewritten pages was not at all the Nancy I thought I'd put there. She had changed during the journey from inside my head. I had failed in my intention.

This might be a good point at which to warn you never to sneer at what it takes to write women's magazine stories. You might believe that they are all rubbish. But just you try writing one. Most people don't realize the specialized techniques involved. To write a story for *Women's Own* or a novel for Gollancz is to do two *different* things but the one isn't by definition *easier* to do than the other. Short stories indeed can be much more difficult to write than novels.

It was my mother's burning ambition that I should get a story published in *The People's Friend* and I'm damned if I was able to do it. I tried and tried but somehow could never get the hang of it. My mother found this difficult to forgive. She certainly never understood.

"Such nice, simple wee stories," she used to say, "I'm sure you could write one if you tried."

One thing I must make clear. I'm talking about letting people read your story *after you have finished writing it.* (Or after you *think* you have finished doing all the work that you can possibly do on it.)

Never, I repeat NEVER allow people to see it at any stage *before* you finish writing it. Lots of people do this and more often than not it turns out to be their Waterloo. They form little self-help groups with friends who are also "interested in writing" or who have "an intelligent appreciation of literature". They all try to bring something along that they have written. Each piece is read out and then chewed over by one and all.

Now the danger in this situation is not that the tyro will not be able to take criticism. If anything he'll take too much and become confused and led further and further away from his original idea and how he wanted to express it. It's a matter of confidence. Creativity is such a sensitive, intuitive, private thing. It needs nursing in secret if it's going to survive. You can get a perfectly good idea. You can get the excitement needed to beaver away and work it out on paper. That excitement, that belief in your story idea, your story characters, that belief in yourself, keeps you going and gets the work *done*.

Or, you can get that idea and immediately hare along to your friend or friends and with one critical word from one of them at that sensitive stage, your idea can wither and die before it has had a chance to properly take root. And your excitement fritters away in uncertainty and lack of confidence. It's not that your friends mean any harm to your writing any more than you mean any harm to theirs. It's simply that creativity doesn't work that way.

Another thing that happens is, you talk your excitement out. You *tell* the story instead of writing it.

That's no use. As John Braine said: "A writer is a person who writes."

# CHAPTER EIGHT

I LEARNED to accept and be grateful for criticism. Most writers when they ask for an opinion of their work are only seeking praise. I wanted praise too and I was secretly furious and hurt when I didn't get it. But I learned to accept what I did get with a stiff upper lip. I began to look at my work with more objectivity and if I thought the criticism was valid I acted on it. I was so determined to become a published writer I would have done anything to help me succeed. When I once told this to a friend she said: "Would you sleep with your publisher?"

This was a non-writer friend and I have since realized that she revealed a very common belief held by people who don't know anything about what it takes to be a creative writer. People think that becoming a writer and getting your work published depends on who you know. Let me assure you that if there is one profession in the world where this dictum does not, definitely does not apply, it is the novelist's profession. I can't speak for films, stage or television. I don't know anything about these things. But with the world of creative fiction I have had some experience.

I've known writers who have had as many as nine books published and they have known innumerable influential people. Yet they've had their tenth book turned down.

The reasons can be varied. The writer could have been trying to change his or her style and try something different and failed in the attempt. The publisher could have bought a book on the same subject and with similar characters the day before. Or it could be a bad time to buy a book of the type offered. There are peaks and troughs of popularity in certain genres. Sometimes war books, for instance, sell like wildfire. Then sales drop away until no publisher can afford the loss involved in buying one. The book might simply have been a lousy idea, indifferently written.

It depends on the market, it depends on budgets but most of all it depends on the book. And, as I've indicated, it's not only beginners but even established writers who find it difficult to get published. He can never let up. You have to realize that you're only as good as your next book. You have to remember that his is one of the most competitive professions in the world.

If only it was as easy as sleeping with your publisher. The truth is that out of the hundreds and hundreds of writers I've now met, known, and known of, I've never heard of one, not one that had her first novel accepted because she slept with her publisher. But in those far-off early days when my friend put that startling question to me I didn't realize what a hard life it was. I took her question seriously. My strict Calvinistic upbringing forced me to answer: "No, I certainly would not!"

It gave me food for secret thought though and in my innocence (and desperation) I dreamed dreams of some handsome fairy prince of a publisher taking a fancy to me (also, of course, recognizing my genius) and waving his magic wand and making me a best-selling author overnight. If any beginner writer is nursing dreams of this nature, my advice is — forget it! The only way to make your dream of getting a novel published come true is to stay awake and work like a creature possessed on it.

I was determined to do whatever I could, anything that was necessary to get my work into acceptable form. So when, at one point — I think it was after I'd finished my fourth attempt at a novel — I saw an advert somewhere that criticism and revision to bring a book up to publishable standards could be done by experts at a price, I was hooked. I rushed my typescript away and was told by letter that the book showed much promise and could be made publishable at a cost of £25. That was a lot of money in those days and it certainly was a fortune to me. I'd never had such a sum in my life. I determined to get it. I knew there was no use asking my parents. They didn't have that kind of money either. Anyway, this was before I'd had a word published and the writing side of my life was never spoken of or in any way taken seriously by my family and friends. My success as a writer seemed within my grasp and by God I wasn't going to let it go.

In great fear and trepidation in case anyone saw me, I went to where a moneylender had an office in the main street in town. As I hovered outside the place trying to pluck up courage to enter, I was nearly dying of shame. But it was more than that. Looking back now, I realize that I was also shrinking from repeating a pattern of instinctual experience that had formed when I was a child.

Regular as clockwork every week I was sent along to one or other of the local shops to ask:

"Could you please give me some butter and bread and tea and sugar and sausages and potatoes and chocolate biscuits?" And I was to tell whoever served me, "My mammy will pay you at the end of the week."

I knew instinctively as I set out for the shop that I was in charge of a vitally important errand. My "antennae" had picked up the urgency from my mother, especially as she watched me from the window as I went along the road. Her back was as straight as ever and her head still had its proud tilt and she would smile and nod to me, encouraging me on. Yet I sensed her anxiety.

Entering the shop I would become lost in a forest of tall people but eventually would manage to crush a path towards a high wooden counter. Above it towered the shop assistant who seemed to always register disapproval and irritation at what I was going to say before I opened my mouth. I sensed looks being exchanged above my head. The boss appeared. The problem I had raised was discussed. Often customers joined in. In an agony of shame and suspense, I waited. If I was at last given the groceries it would be with a lecture about how they were giving them to me this time but if they didn't get paid by the end of the week, it would be the last time.

My anxiety was increased a hundredfold because I knew that they might not get paid at the end of the week. It might not be their turn and I would have to go back with some trumped-up excuse that hadn't a chance of being believed. The complicated and fearful juggling match my mother played with money had to be seen to be believed. I don't know if my mother's grand, impulsive nature made my father insecure and overcautious and that's why he didn't give her much housekeeping money or whether he was just being rotten. But I'll never forget the week my mother found that he had earned nine pounds and only given her three. (She had either rifled his pockets or read his diary. He never failed to record everything meticulously in his diary no matter how often this habit was the means of bringing him to rough justice.)

Anyway, my mother who seemed to live for the moment, would visibly relax when she spotted me tottering triumphantly along the road with a full basket of groceries. The whole atmosphere of the house would change. I would sense the air light and intoxicating the moment I stepped over the threshold. My mother would sing as she strode around making the dinner.

If by some awful chance I failed in my errand to the shops, the house would become as tight as a drum with anxiety and I would be sent off again to try another shop or, failing that, a neighbour or friend. It was better, though, if a shop saved the day because that meant chocolate biscuits.

Strange as it may seem this matter of the choclate biscuits is important to me as a writer. It helps me to understand the apparently stupid, reckless, self-indulgent, spendthrift ways of some people who have been deprived. It's painful to be without the basic necessities and it does things not only to the body but to the spirit. There's the suspenseful anxiety, for instance, the shame that can't but must be faced of someone coming to the door when you've nothing to offer them, not even a cup of tea.

These are pains, these are anxieties that cause a wretched craving that, at the first opportunity, must be reassured and comforted away. What comforted my mother and me was chocolate biscuits. We really wolfed them whenever we got the chance.

It's an awful lot easier to keep an even keel and budget sensibly when at the same time you are secure in being able to continuously enjoy modest comforts and necessities. It was always a hunger and a burst with us.

With nothing but this memory bank to draw on my visit to the moneylender was an agony indeed. However, so strong was my desperation to succeed as a writer, I forced myself into the place. A man with certain Fagin-like features came to the counter and I told him in trembling voice how I needed £25 to get my novel published and would he please give it to me and I promised to pay it back as soon as I could.

He said to go away home and ask my father.

So you see, there are decent and kindly moneylenders and I'll be forever grateful to that one. Not that I went home and asked my father. As I've said, I knew that was no use. I just went home and shut myself in the bathroom and had a tragic brokenhearted howl.

But I got over it and soon I was hard at work on my fifth novel.

It sounds easy saying it in one sentence like that. The truth is, that time in the bathroom wasn't the only time I cried. I used to collapse over my notebooks and weep with sheer hopelessness and exhaustion. I used to think: "I can't do it. It's just not in me to become a writer. No matter how hard I try I just haven't got the talent. There's no use pretending, I have to face the truth. I haven't got what it takes. I'll never do it."

Then, from somewhere deep inside me would come a ripple of indignation and a *thrawness* as my mother would say. And I would suddenly sit up and think: "No, damn it, I *will* do it! I will! If it takes me all my life, I'll get a book published — even if it happens the day before I die — I'll manage it!"

But I didn't manage it with my fifth book, either.

"All right," I thought, "I'll change my tactics. Maybe I'm making the mistake of aiming too high to begin with. Maybe I'm starting with something too big. Right, then. I'll try starting at the other end."

So I wrote a letter to a woman's magazine's letter page and HALLELUJAH I got it published! I'll never forget opening the magazine on the street (I couldn't wait until I got home) and there was my letter, my very own words in print. A few days later I received a cheque for five pounds.

By this time my first marriage had ended and I had married again. My new husband was a widower with a young son and the letter was a heartfelt cry about the difficult situation of second wives and stepmothers. This happened to be the subject the magazine had asked for letters to be on that week.

About the same time I discovered the Glasgow Corporation ran a course on "Literary Appreciation". The man who took the course was a Mr Scoular and many a potential writer has gone through his hands and been grateful to him. The weekly meetings were held in a large hall which was always packed. Mr Scoular would begin by giving a talk. All that I can remember of those was that in one he said that good journalism was when a paper said that ten thousand troops of the army of the USSR crossed the border of —— at ——. Bad journalism was when the paper said that Red hordes had overrun ——.

After the talk he would read out an article or short story written by one of the audience. Then anyone in the audience who had an opinion about the piece would voice it. Finally, Mr Scoular gave his own views. I always thought his criticism was objective, constructive and fair. You had to be tough, however, to survive some of the things the audience said.

I had a friend who put in a story. It had quite a rough ride and she never wrote a story again in her life. This was a great pity because she had writing talent. To this day I daren't mention Mr Scoular's name to her (and the poor man's dead and buried now) without her erupting in bitterness, hatred and resentment against him.

But my friend didn't fail to become a writer because of Mr Scoular or indeed anyone in that audience who said anything about her story. She has many excellent and indeed lovable personality traits. She just didn't have the right characteristics to be an author.

# CHAPTER NINE

I PLUGGED the stepmother-stepchild theme again in a story that I submitted to Mr Scoular's class.

It got a mixed reception at the class but the general consensus was that it was extremely moving. I now owned a typewriter and I typed a fresh copy and sent it winging its way to a glossy women's magazine. It came back with what I realize now was a most encouraging letter. To me, then, it was just another failure.

Perhaps, I thought, I was still aiming too high. I decided to organize an attack on D.C. Thomson's small magazines. First of all, I bought them: *People's Friend, Family Star, Red Letter, Secrets* — the lot. I read them from cover to cover and I hated them. I absolutely despised them. But I struggled with my emotions once I'd got a few of my stories returned from these same publications.

There was no use me slanging D.C. Thomson's stories. The fact was, I hadn't the expertise to write them. I also faced up to the fact that there was a place for the romantic short stories they contained. And the romantic thriller serials. As well as their entertainment value they provided an escape for working-class girls in monotonous dead-end jobs. The chances were, nothing exciting or thrilling or truly romantic ever happened to them. Nor were they ever masters of their own destinies. (Especially after they got married and especially in Scotland!) In these stories however, they could identify with heroines who made thrilling, exciting things happen all the time; and the heroes were so strong yet so tender, and romantic.

There were a lot worse things in the world than D.C. Thomson's stories, I decided.

I buckled down to make a serious study of each of the magazines. I even examined the advertising. Actually this is important when doing market study. From the kind of advertising, you can deduce what social class of reader the publication is aimed at, and what age group, and whether married or single; what kind of clothes are worn, what kind of jobs are held.

The problem pages and agony columns are also helpful not only for finding out the type of person who reads the magazine (and remember, the reader has to sympathize and identify with the story characters) but as a source of story ideas.

I gave the stories themselves my most concentrated attention. I analysed them but not in the same way that stories were picked over and turned inside out and upside down in the classes I'd attended at the university extra-mural department. Now I was finding out practical, useful things like how the authors caught the reader's interest at the beginning of their stories (the interest hook), exactly how they sustained that interest (the conflict and the suspense), and how they ended the stories. (The dénouement which had to be, for the most part, happy. Or at least, hopeful or leaving the reader with the feeling — well, it was the best thing that could have happened in the circumstances.)

I analysed each story with a writer's eye — with the sole view of doing it myself.

Just look at some short story beginnings to see what I mean about that interest hook for instance. The interest must be caught right away in the first paragraph or if possible the first sentence. Usually this is done by stating the story problem or some aspect of it. For instance, one story of mine which was published in a Sunday newspaper began with the sentence:

"Every time Joe McGouran passed Jail Square he thought of his father and prayed that no one would ever find out."

A story for radio and a woman's magazine began with:

"Guy stared at her, his eyes wary like a stranger. 'I always believed you were different underneath. Maybe it was just wishful thinking.'"

Another for radio and a magazine started with:

"William Temple was a good man — a pillar of society — and no one knew it better than he."

If you don't start by indicating an aspect of the problem you must catch the interest with the character or by a vivid setting, situation or atmosphere.

All stories must grab the interest of the reader in some way. Literary stories are no exception. D.H. Lawrence's "The Witch à la Mode" starts with:

"When Bernard Coutts alighted at East Croydon he knew he was tempting providence."

A Kafka story called "Metamorphosis" begins with:

"As Gregor Samsa awoke one morning from uneasy dreams he found himself transformed in his bed into a gigantic insect."

A Maugham story, "The Unconquered", starts:

"He came back to the kitchen. The man was still on the floor, lying where he had hit him, and his face was bloody."

In a short story every word must count. There obviously isn't enough room to stretch oneself as there is in the novel and there certainly isn't room for a long preamble. And you must make the most of every situation. In order to do this it helps to use the shortest time span possible, the fewest characters and the closest relationships.

But I found even with the romantic magazine stories I had to approach them in much the same way as I would eventually approach the writing of a novel. Something would spark off an emotional response in me. I would feel amusement, resentment, pity, love, fear, anger, curiosity, compassion. Or I would observe emotions and tune into them in other people. Then I would shape this reaction or emotion into the form, the technique of the short story.

Most of the magazine short stories I studied were made up of a problem, conflict arising out of the problem, and the solution of the problem. With this in mind I wrote a story called "Waiting for the Crowdens". I thought it might be the type that would appeal to *My Weekly*. It seemed to me that this magazine at that time specialized in quite good emotional-type stories and it was one of D.C. Thomson's publications which aimed at older, married, and more comfortably off readers.

The story spark came from an emotion aroused in me by my father-in-law. The old man had lived with us in worsening stages of senility since we'd been married. Sometimes he would be quite normal and capable. At other times, without warning he would do awful things. Looking back I find some of them funny although they were not quite so hilarious at the time. Like when I was trying to sell our house in Cardonald. I had put a very glowing advert in the paper about the house and a whole crowd of people came to see it. In my anxiety to make sure there would be no hitches I had worked like a slave scrubbing and polishing so that the place looked its best. Eventually I had about two dozen potential buyers crowded into my sitting-room and I had been extolling the virtues of the house before showing them around when suddenly my father-in-law shuffled in, rubbing his hands, and announced to me as if no one else were in the room:

"I'm away to the pub but I've left the electric fire on in my room to make it look as if it's warm!"

The next night I was leading a very prim and sedate couple upstairs to view the bedrooms when halfway we were stopped in our tracks by the vision of my father-in-law emerging from the bathroom in his shirt-tails and carrying a chamber pot.

"Evening!" he said and carried on upstairs. I had no option but to follow him with the now horrified lady and gentleman in tow.

It took a long time to sell that perfectly good house but I eventually managed it and at nearly 100 per cent profit.

But to get back to "Waiting for the Crowdens". I was expecting

49

friends for a meal and wanted to give them a nice evening. But the problem was my father-in-law who always ate with us and who was now dropping his food all over the table and slavering and generally making a terrible mess. The poor soul couldn't help it. I realized that and I think I can truthfully say that I never once criticized him or complained to him or indeed ever said an unkind word to him — certainly not that I'm aware of. But it could make one feel physically sick at times. It could also be excrutiatingly embarrassing when guests were in. So when I was expecting these particular guests, who had never been to our house before, I found myself in a dilemma. It's a long time ago now and I can't remember exactly, but I suppose I wanted to impress them and I was afraid my father-in-law would show me up.

After much nailbiting, worry and indecision, I eventually gave him his meal in his room. I felt horribly guilty about it. Although looking back now I can see I had absolutely no need. The old man and I got on well and I nursed him as best I could through thick and thin for years before he died. But I did feel distraught and guilty about giving him his dinner in his room and when I came to write "Waiting for the Crowdens" I decided to use this emotion, and to base the story on this incident.

Now we come to the technique bit.

During the telling of a short story, either the situation in which the characters are placed undergoes a change, or the characters adapt to fit the situation. In either case, something must change. If no change occurs then it is a sketch not a story. A short story deals with a particular incident, a brief space of time in the life of a character. It highlights one small but telling part. It illuminates rather than develops. (A novel develops.) So, keeping all the things I've said about the short story in mind, I set to thinking of how I could adapt the real-life emotion, characters and situation to the medium of the short story.

First, I thought of how the closer the relationship of the character was, the stronger the story drama was likely to be. So I thought — right, a father/daughter relationship is closer than a father-in-law/daughter-in-law relationship. So that's what I'll make it. Then it occurred to me that it might be even better, especially for a woman's magazine, to make it a mother rather than a father. So a mother it became in my mind. So, it was going to be a story about this woman — let's call her Moira — who is expecting people to dinner and her mother is going to create a problem.

Now, there's another part of technique to remember, and this applies to the novel as well as the short story. You must make the most of every situation And push everyone to their limits. So instead of making it just any old dinner for instance, I made it a Christmas dinner. You can see immediately how this strengthens the dilemma and enables me to make the most of the emotions involved.

Now I've got to think of the characters in more detail. I've got to get their motivations clear in my mind. Instead of making Moira just a harassed housewife, instead of making her just a little embarrassed, I push her into much stronger emotions.

I begin my story by stating the problem in the first sentence. I set the scene, at the same time revealing Moira's character. Then, to keep up the suspense as well as feeding in more information, I go into flashback. I don't make the ending exactly what you'd call a happy one but it is as it should be — that is, it is intended to make the reader feel: Yes, that is the best that could have happened in the circumstances.

# CHAPTER TEN

I HAD MANY stories published after that and in all sorts of styles: romantic, humorous, crime, literary; and I had quite a few broadcast. But how can I tell you of the joy I felt when I had that first story accepted? It wasn't the sight of my words in print or hearing them read by an actress on radio. Although these things were thrilling enough.

I'd done it. I'd cracked it. I'd shown them. I'd won!

Yet it was more than that. I had such a desperate need to reach out to someone. Steinbeck said:

> A writer out of loneliness is trying to communicate like a distant star sending signals. He isn't telling or teaching or ordering. Rather he seeks to establish a relationship of meaning, of feeling, of observing.
>
> We are lonesome animals. We spend all life trying to be less lonesome. One of our ancient methods is to tell a story begging the listener to say — and to feel —
>
> "Yes, that's the way it is, or at least that's the way I feel it. You're not as lonely as you thought."

I determined to consolidate my success. I'd get a story into every magazine I aimed for — even if it was just the once — just to prove to myself that I could do it. So I tried other D.C. Thomson magazines and I got other stories published in them before moving on to bigger publications. But don't imagine I simply sent in stories after that and got them accepted. It's never that easy. I sent in stories and I got them back. Time after time after time. What kept me going now was the belief that if I had done it once I could do it again.

I must say that the editors of those first small magazines were very helpful. I'm not the first and I won't be the last writer they have nursed along. Nursed along is perhaps too soft a term, though. If you couldn't take straight-from-the-shoulder criticism you fell by the wayside and that was the end of you as far as they were concerned.

Frank Sinatra and his "I did it my way" would have been no use to them. You had to learn to do it *their way*. The self-discipline involved was invaluable and is something else every writer needs to acquire before coming to write the novel. This training in self-discipline was really put to the test when I started writing romantic thriller serials for D.C. Thomson. Instalment by instalment they kept me right by pointing out exactly, and in no uncertain terms, where I was going wrong.

I learned how to make action spring from character. It all depended on the type of characters you started with because characters had to respond *characteristically* to whatever happened to them. What I did after I'd thought up my characters for those serials was to put them into a starting situation of menace, challenge them and let them take it from there.

A whole new world of possibilities began to open up before me and in more ways than one.

It is D.C. Thomson's policy after they buy a few stories from you, and have established a working relationship, to invite you to meetings with their editors. An editor would come up to Glasgow for instance, and from his hotel base he would invite an author to morning coffee, another for afternoon tea. The more established you were, the more lavish the hospitality offered. You graduated from coffee and biscuits, to afternoon tea and sandwiches, to lunch, and then to dinner. The highest accolade was when you were invited to come through to Dundee to be shown around their offices and meet all their editors. You were booked in at a hotel and had dinner, and breakfast, and morning coffee and lunch and afternoon tea. The whole works!

At Christmas they sent you a tartan tin of shortbread.

I was still at the morning coffee stage when I was told by letter that they were starting a new magazine — a glossy type magazine — and the editor of it wished to meet me to discuss the contribution I could make. This was terribly exciting. To be in at the beginning of a new magazine — a big, glossy magazine! But, as I've said before, it's never easy to get a story accepted. Failure was the constant spectre at my elbow. Determined to succeed however, I set off early for the hotel armed with my pencil and notebook to jot down every pearl of wisdom that fell from the editor's lips. It wasn't so much — what to do — I had to find out. With D.C. Thomson it was more important to know what *not* to do.

They were a funny firm. They had these strict taboos they couldn't even bring themselves to lay on the line. You had the most awful job to find out, and usually only did so by trial and error; for instance — no story in which the heroine smoked a cigarette was ever accepted. Drink was definitely not on. And you could really do yourself a professional injury with kissing and canoodling.

Of course, for all I knew they might be breaking new ground with this latest magazine. It was imperative for me to find out. I arrived too early for my appointment and sat with notebook on

53

knee and pen poised at the ready. I was slightly nonplussed when the editor eventually arrived. Instead of the usual father-type figure, he was a comparatively young and rather attractive man. Quickly recovering, however, I got straight down to business.

"About sex," I burst out. "How far can I go?"

His eyes twinkled. "How far do you want to go, love?"

It didn't even occur to me to smile. I just pressed earnestly on with my enquiries. I've always taken my job as a writer very seriously.

It turned out that they wanted emotional stories for that magazine exactly of the type I had been writing for *My Weekly* and BBC Radio. This suited me fine. I'd written lots of other types by now (and not only for D.C. Thomson); you name it, I'd had a go at it. But I preferred the serious emotional kind.

The funny thing was, though, by this time my personal life was going through a ghastly phase and I'm damned if I could write anything but either suspense thrillers or humour. There is an interesting point here. Just think of all the clowns and comedians who have suffered from depression or committed suicide. I've come to the conclusion that you can only make use of the real harrowing stuff in retrospect — once you're 'safely removed from the intimate personal experience of it. I suppose that's what Tolstoy means with his definition of Art. Wordsworth no doubt realized it too when he spoke of poetry being an overflow of powerful feelings but added:

> It takes its origin from emotion recollected in tranquillity: the emotion is contemplated till, by a species of reaction, the tranquillity gradually disappears and an emotion, kindred to that which was before the subject of contemplation, is gradually produced, and does itself actually exist in the mind.

That can be difficult and harrowing enough but from a retrospective situation at least you're working from a position of safety and physical strength. It's like being in the centre of a whirlpool or a tornado. It's possible to conjure up a vivid and exciting description of it long afterwards when you're sitting in the quiet safety of your room. At the time of being in the whirlpool or the tornado all you can do is struggle to survive.

I was struggling with my father-in-law who by this time was doing things like trying to set the house on fire in the middle of the night. He seemed to be all right when my husband was in during the day (although my husband at that time went out quite a lot with his friends during the day so he didn't really see all that much of his father). At night when my husband was out working as a taxi-driver, the old man completely lost not only his mind but also control of his bladder and bowels. Every evening he disintegrated as a human being. I had to continuously struggle to lift him and lay him. He used to fall out of bed, fall from his chair in front of the fire, fall downstairs, get outside wearing only his pyjamas and fall in the street.

Apart from the physical toll it took out of me, I became very depressed. It was so sad to look at the photograph on the wall of the handsome young man the old man had once been and to witness his terrible disintegration. Fortunately, he didn't seem to know about it. He used to chat away quite happily (and loudly) in the middle of the night to friends long dead. Sometimes he'd get angry with them and shout at me to take them away. But next morning he never remembered anything about it.

Perhaps it was understandable that my husband never believed me that anything was wrong. All the same, our marriage began to deteriorate and not only because of the strains imposed by my father-in-law. No doubt I was as much to blame as my husband. As I said to my mother there are two sides to every story. I couldn't stand a couple of his friends. He couldn't stand my mother. She couldn't stand him. Although eventually they became friends and he was kind to her and she became very fond of him. My husband and I eventually became friends too. But I was drained, both physically and emotionally. I took a heart attack and then I had to go to hospital for an operation.

When I returned home and buckled down to write that serious emotional story for the new magazine, I just couldn't do it. I found myself writing a light-hearted piece of nonsense. It was a very long time before I could tackle a serious story again.

When I did, I wrote a story about an old man's dying. Another very successful one was about a woman who has left her husband and is wandering the streets of Glasgow with her children, trying to find a place to live. A third which was published in this country and several countries overseas and was also given repeat broadcasts was about a woman who was faced with the decision of bringing her mother who was in need of care, to live with her, or putting her into an institution.

I'd now had a great many short stories published. My real goal in life however had always been and still was to become a novelist. I didn't regret my time writing short stories. I regarded it as my apprenticeship as a writer. And it had bolstered my sagging confidence. Now I was able to spur myself on by repeating to myself that if I could get short work into print, I could get long work into print. It was just a matter of sticking at it and learning the appropriate techniques.

With this in mind I travelled down to Derbyshire to attend my first Writers' School at the Hayes Conference Centre in Swanwick. This is where I met my dear wee friend John Maloney. I can still see him hirpling about excitedly (he had a club foot) among all the writers in that beautiful place.

I was overcome with hysterical excitement myself. Here, at last, I was among my own kind. Here were writers — three hundred of them, all bursting to talk about writing. Gloriously, gloriously happy times! I've gone every year since with the same deliriously happy excitement, and I have left at the end of the week with my face red and swollen after tearful goodbyes to so many dearly-loved friends.

That first year, one of the lecturers was Alexander Cordell. I was so moved by his lecture and the excerpts he read from one of his books that afterwards I left the lecture hall and went straight to my bedroom and wept with — I don't know — the sheer emotional appreciation of it all.

Later, outside on the sunny lawn, I plucked up courage to approach Cordell. I spilled out all my troubles (everyone does this to everyone all the time at Swanwick) about how I'd written five novels and none of them were any use and how I desperately wanted to write books that would get published.

True to what I now know is the Swanwick tradition, he gave me his help and advice in a most generous and unstinting way. At one point in our conversation he asked:

"Where exactly are you from, Margaret? What is the background you know best?"

I told him I was from Glasgow. My original background was working-class. I'd been brought up in the tenements of Glasgow.

"Well," he said, "you go back from Swanwick and sit down and, with as much courage and honesty as you can muster, write a novel about Glasgow and about life in the Glasgow tenements."

I stared at him in astonishment. It had never occurred to me to do that.

# CHAPTER ELEVEN

ON MY WAY home from Swanwick I closed my eyes and drifted back to the jungle of Glasgow streets.

For some time now I'd been living in a middle to upper middle-class place outside of Glasgow, called Bearsden. There were no Glasgow-type tenements there. People lived in roomy terrace-houses (our terrace house had six rooms and also a kitchen big enough to eat in and a scullery and a bathroom) or neat bungalows or large villas. The streets were lined with trees and within minutes you could be away by car to beautiful countryside. Everybody had a car. There was a car park — thickly screened by trees — at the back of the shops in the centre of Bearsden. The Centre was also referred to as "The Village" and we lived just along from the shops.

I had never seen a housewife going about her business in that place looking harassed. They all seemed so well-fed, so well-dressed, so sure of themselves in their comfortable routines. Their lives (or so it appeared) were a continuous round of coffee mornings during which they admired each other's home-baking and swapped recipes, or managed to keep them secret. Somebody's new curtains were noted and criticized. The previous day's golf or evening's bridge was verbally replayed. The merits and demerits of new fashions in clothes or furnishings were argued about. Keep-fit efforts, slimming failures and successes were giggled at or sighed over. Diets were discussed eagerly and *endlessly*.

Looking after oneself and cushioning oneself from any disturbing ripples in life had been mastered to a fine art. The main object in existence — apart from looking after oneself — was to keep up appearances and to be seen to fit in to the accepted pattern and conventions.

I eventually wrote a book called *The Prisoner* which I set in Bearsden and in which I delve beneath the surface appearances of respectability there. Of this book one reviewer said many complimentary things but ended by remarking:

"I don't know what they'll think of it in Bearsden though!"

I didn't wait to find out. But I'm jumping the gun.

I must return to that train journey from Swanwick. There I was, allowing myself to drift back in time to life in the real Glasgow and as I did so, to more and more "tune in" to the feelings, to the essence of the place and to the people who had lived there. At first vague images of people and scenes floated into my head. Gradually

I began to feel my way into them. More and more I concentrated my senses on them.

I heard children singing and playing in the streets. The sound of their peaver scraped close to my ear. Their ball thumped rhythmically.

"One-two-three-a-leary, four-five-six-a-leary, seven-eight-nine-a-leary, ten-a-leary postman!"

Women puffed and hustled along, each clutching a shopping-bag heavy as a sack of coal in one hand and a purse in the other. Groups of women laughed and enjoyed a good blether (chat) in shops, in close-mouths (tunnel-like entrances to tenement buildings) or at street corners. Coal horses clopped along led by black-faced coalmen bawling:

"Co — o — ee, any o — o — ee fo — o — ee! Co — o — ee!"

I smelled kipper cooking, and sausages.

The close was draughty and had a damp chill as I entered it and went skipping up the stairs. A symphony of sounds whirled around me. From behind closed and open doors came laughter and angry shouting.

"Wullie! If you don't stop tormentin' that wean, ah'm gonni murder yi!"

My mother playing "The Old Rugged Cross" on the piano. Alvar Liddell on the wireless telling everyone the news. Someone jauntily singing:

"All the nice girls love a sailor, all the nice girls love a tar, — tum — tee — tum — tee — tum — tee — tum, — tum — tee — tum — tee — tum — tee — tum — Ship ahoy! Ship ahoy!"

Despite the cold winter's air, the warm, crowded, cheery bustle of it all. . . .

The more I concentrated on it, the more intensely I felt it. I felt it in my bones. But how to make a novel of it? Where did I start? During the next few days and weeks I gave my thoughts and instincts free rein. I also went back and wandered about the streets I'd once known so well.

My mother and father still lived in the same corporation housing scheme in Balornock although not in the same flat. My brother, now married to his childhood sweetheart, lived down the hill in a room and kitchen in Springburn. My aunt and uncle and cousins also lived in a room and kitchen in an old tenement in Springburn and their lavatory was also out on the landing. This tiny window-less and lightless lavatory had to be shared by several other families and if you weren't very nippy on your feet it wasn't always easy to get in there. If nature called and the place was engaged there just had to be some other way to relieve the problem.

My Aunt Meg had what she called "The Throne". In the room there was a walk-in cupboard which had a curtain instead of a door. In the cupboard, as well as everything from old paint brushes to old mattresses, there was a zinc pail. This was what my Aunt referred to when she told me kindly:

"Don't worry, hen. Just away through and use The Throne!"

She suffered terribly with asthma and had to puff up and down the stairs to empty the pail when she could catch the lavatory at a vacant moment (which was probably only in the middle of the night).

I never heard her complain about that or anything. In fact she was always saying how lucky she was having the Co-op so handy at the corner. Her neighbours, she insisted, were absolute "gems". If she wasn't well, or if she needed a loan of a wee drop sugar, all she had to do was knock on the wall of her kitchen cupboard and Nelly from the next close would hear her and come to the rescue.

Aunt Meg had a pawky sense of humour that was only bettered by my Uncle Dode's hilarious one. He was my mother's brother and he had her marvellous spirit. Even after he went blind, he could keep you in stitches. His health steadily deteriorated but I remember my mother and I, on our way to visit him, met the doctor coming out of my uncle's house. By this time, as I say, Uncle Dode was blind and in pain yet the doctor as he emerged from the house was laughing.

"I felt really depressed before I went in there," he told my mother, "but he always manages to cheer me up!"

When my uncle was lying on his deathbed and my parents and I went to see him, my father sighed and said:

"The last time we met, Dode, I was the one who was ill and you were visiting me."

"Aye, Sam," my uncle managed. "But when I came to see you I brought you a bottle of whisky!"

It was strange, looking back, how I remembered so much laughter. The poorer, the more distressing the circumstances, the stronger the sense of humour there seemed to be. There was a strong sense of community too, family feelings of loyalty and compassion and the recognition of responsibility to help one another that spilled far beyond one's immediate family. I wasn't idealizing or being sentimental about the people and the background. I was looking back with a clear and honest eye. In my experience, that is how the people were.

I remember, for instance, the McLellands downstairs from us. They had a big family and Mr McLelland (through no fault of his own) was unemployed. One time when my father was on night shift a burglar tried to get in our door. My mother banged on the floor with a poker. It wakened Mr McLelland and, taking it as a sign that help was needed, he never even stopped to put on his trousers. He rushed upstairs in his shirt-tails to see what was wrong. On learning from my mother that the man he had passed on the stairs had tried to break into our house, Mr McLelland turned tail and raced after him. I was only a child at the time but I recall with perfect clarity watching out of the front room window and seeing Mr McLelland's half naked body and long hairy legs flying along the road in pursuit of his quarry. He punched the living daylights out of him when he caught him.

Eventually the McLellands couldn't pay their rent and had to "do a moonlight". The coalman or someone had loaned them a horse and cart. They piled the cart as best they could with all their worldly possessions. Then they climbed on top and the whole thing trundled away.

There was at that time what was known as "the back road to Auchinairn". It was hardly more than a lane and it ran between the hospital mortuary and some high bushes behind which were fields and a few derelict farm buildings. It was in one of these buildings — probably an old barn — that the McLellands sought shelter. After that, their old neighbours, including my mother, used to take turns about every week to walk to the back road with a jug of soup or whatever they could manage to scrape up. I remember my mother taking me with her one night and Mrs McLelland coming to the door in her nightdress. She was carrying a lantern. I'll never forget how ill she looked and how her nightdress billowed out in the cold wind. And I had the impression of the children somewhere in the darkness behind her. I was only a child myself but I felt instinctively the terrible deprivation the family must have been suffering there. Mrs McLelland died soon afterwards, of malnutrition it was said. Not long after her death her son Robert was taken to the infirmary. He was about my age, perhaps a little younger. What I remember about him is his pale delicate face, his sad eyes and his too-big "parish" jacket and trousers. Even after all these years his face floats before my mind's eye like a ghost. My mother and I visited him regularly and he always used to cling on to the neck of her blouse. She would cradle him in her arms and nurse him like a baby.

One day he asked her: "Mrs Thomson, am I going to die?"

The doctor had already told my mother that although the appendectomy had been successful, the child was so undernourished he hadn't the strength to survive.

My mother said: "Don't worry. son. All it means is you'll be seeing your mammy again."

He did die and there seemed no doubt that his death was caused by malnutrition. It seems incredible that within my living memory such things could happen. But they did.

I remembered everything — the laughter and the tears. But I was still groping with how best to fashion my material into a novel.

Eventually I got down to business. I got myself organized with main characters. I chose characters that were as different to one another as possible. Contrast and conflict are essential. Even in his earliest days, Sir Walter Scott realized this.

> When I was a child, indeed for some years after, my amusement was in supposing to myself a set of persons engaged in various scenes which contrasted them with each other, and I remember to this day the accuracy with which my childish imagination worked.

Conflict has to be engendered because without conflict there's no story. I also kept in mind what I had learned from my short story writing. Clashes and episodes are always more striking when they happen among relatives or close friends and lovers. I also knew by this time that conflict was achieved by creating an important desire or requirement and putting in the way of its accomplishment all the obstruction you can reasonably introduce. You had to make sure that characters were truly trapped in the conflict, that, being the type of people they were, no alternatives were open to them.

So I had to think of characters and conflict. I also had to decide when — in exactly what year — my story would start and exactly where it would be set. I knew it was going to be set in the city of Glasgow but where in Glasgow? In what street? In what house? And why?

It's not possible to say what one thinks of first and what second, etc. You're just thinking about everything all the time and everything gradually becomes clearer and falls into place. At the same time, it becomes more complicated and one has to start taking voluminous notes. Let me explain.

Once I decided to start my story in 1936 I had to check in the local reference library what was going on, not only in Glasgow but in the world in general in 1936. Not everything in the world, you understand, just the things that my characters would know about or be interested in. What they would know most about and be most interested in of course would be what was going on and what affected them in their own city. One way I found out what was going on was by reading newspapers of the time. Once you start doing a bit of research like this, one thing leads to another and it's

61

amazing how what you discover helps with your character-building and plotting. For instance, I discovered (or was reminded) that the big things in Glasgow every year were: 1) the Govan Fair; 2) the Orange Walk; 3) the Glasgow Fair Fortnight.

As I read first of all about the Govan Fair I was intrigued by the history of it and the vivid images it brought to mind, the pageantry, the decorated floats, the crowds, the excitement. I began to feel myself into it. I became one of the people there. No, not only one, I flittered about inside different people, men, women and children. I was up there on one of the floats waving down at the crowd. I was crushing and jumping among the crowd, cheering and waving back.

I was away. This was it. The book was taking life. But wait. I had been told at Swanwick that it was a good idea to start a book just before a big event. So I decided to start my book in Govan (a district of Glasgow) just before the annual fair, in the middle of my characters' preparations for it.

But what characters?

Now I come to what is for me the most important part of creative writing.

# CHAPTER TWELVE

PROUST SAID that characterization was "the breaking down of observed people and the putting together again". From the breakdown of one observed character you can put together at least a dozen fiction characters each of whom is different from the other. You take one main characteristic (more if necessary — there can be no hard and fast rules) and you exaggerate that, and to it you add other, different characteristics, some perhaps from another observed character, some chosen from your imagination to strengthen the impression you want to create. An important purpose of characterization is to make the reader feel strongly in a specific way towards the person whom you are characterizing.

Scott drew a bitter portrait of his father in one book and a pleasanter one in another. Stendhal, in one of his manuscripts, noted the names of the persons who had suggested his characters. Dickens portrayed his father.in Mr Micawber and Leigh Hunt in Harold Skimpole. Turgenev stated that he could not create a character at all unless as a starting point he could fix his imagination on a living person. And he said that it is only if you have a definite person in your mind that you can give vitality and idiosyncrasy to your own creation.

But, as I've previously pointed out, the writer does not copy the originals. Copying isn't creating. The writer takes what he wants from people. He takes a few traits that have caught his attention, a turn of mind that has interested him and fired his imagination, something that has aroused his feelings. From these things the writer constructs his characters. It's a matter of sheer chance whether he chooses his models from people with whom he's intimately connected or not. It's often enough for him to have caught a glimpse of someone in a railway station or chatted to him for a few minutes at a party. He only needs that tiny fertile substratum. He can build on it using his own experience of life, his knowledge of human nature and his intuition.

Everyone is affected by joy, fear, love and hate. Everyone is attached to his own opinions. Everyone has an infinite quality of mercy for his own failings and weaknesses. Each fiction character must have something of those contradictions to appear original and true to life. Only by opposites in character can drama be drawn and suspense created, only by a clash of wills can character develop and demonstrate itself.

I mulled over character-creation. Already, seething noisily, rumbustiously around me (in my imagination) were the people of the Glasgow tenements as I had known them. Not people with faces that I'd ever seen. But people I sensed I knew from the inside.

But I had to have main characters, and one in particular through which the reader could continuously identify.

I bought myself some school jotters and in front of the first one I wrote (after long and painful thought and studying of telephone directories): CATRIONA MUNRO.

Inside the jotter I made a list which ran like this:

Name — Catriona Munro
Address —
Age at beginning of story —
Height —
Weight —
Colouring:  Hair —
            Complexion —
            Eyes —
Physical characteristics and general description —
Mannerisms —
What kind of clothes does she wear? —
What kind of food does she eat? —
Does she drink or/and smoke? (If so, what) —
Background and home life —
Main personality traits (good and bad) —

Once I'd filled in my character's name I then came to her address and was forced to start imagining her setting. I thought of my own home when I was a girl in Balornock. I remembered the narrow strip of kitchenette with its two inconveniently high shelves. There were no kitchen units in those days to keep everything dust and fly free. At least, not for us. My mother used to keep food in the only thing in the kitchenette that had a door on it — the oven. There was a wooden chair jammed in between the zinc boiler and the coal bunker. I used to sit there and have my breakfast off the top of the boiler before going to school or work. My mother and father slept on a bed settee in the living-room where we usually ate. It was a small room and at night the table and chairs had to be jammed back so that the settee could be opened and the bed made ready. I slept on a bed-settee in the front room, (which meant I couldn't go to bed early if my mother had visitors in). My young brother slept in the bedroom. That was when we had the downstairs flat.

Upstairs lived Mrs Davidson, a mountain of a woman who liked

64

nothing better than to sit at her front-room window watching the world go by, at the same time making comments about it. Some of these were quite scathing like when she saw one man passing and remarked, "Look at that lazy sod. He's never done a stroke of work since he's retired!"

Our front room, like our living-room, might have been depressingly shabby and drab had it not been for the colourful riot of Christmas cards, toffee tins and biscuit tins decorating every available surface. My mother liked a pretty picture and if it happened to be on a Christmas card or a toffee tin she saw no reason why it should not give her (and, she firmly believed, everyone else who entered her house) continuing pleasure. We never took our Christmas cards down.

Embarrassed by this eccentricity I used to make desperate attempts to remove them before one of my friends arrived. But in a clash of wills with my mother there was seldom any doubt as to who would come out victorious. My mother had a strong independent spirit and as she often said, would bend the knee to no one.

"Even if the Queen walked in that door," she used to say, "I wouldn't bend the knee to her. I'd just treat her the same as any other decent body."

Thinking of my mother really took me back. I didn't just see that house in my imagination, I was there again. I was plunged into the gloom of the windowless lobby. The draught was rattling the letter-box. I could hear my father's voice raised in heated argument about politics with another dungareed railwayman in the living-room. In the front room my mother was sitting at the piano, chin up, chest heaving in a rendering of: "If I can help somebody, as I go along. If I can help somebody with a word or song. . . ."

My brother Audley was sitting on the chair in the kitchenette reading and getting the heat from the gas cooker.

There was a smell of newly washed clothes and leek soup.

I decided to make Catriona Munro's home a bottom flat tenement but not in Balornock which was the north side of the city. It was more convenient for the purpose of my story if she lived over the Govan side. I thought up an imaginary place called Farmbank which I visualized as a sort of extension of Govan — a corporation housing scheme tacked on to the Govan conurbation of very much older tenements around the shipyards. (I realize now that I didn't need to make it a fictitious place. I could quite easily have used a real place — somewhere over that end of the city.)

I broke off from filling up the notebook about Catriona's character to start another notebook about Farmbank. I drew a street-map of the place and wrote in imaginary names of streets. I pin-pointed Catriona's street and close and flat. On a separate page I drew a map of the house. (By the way, in Scotland flats are referred to as houses.)

My imagination had taken over. I was creating something and this process continued. I wasn't drawing or describing my old home in Balornock. This was Catriona Munro's home in Farmbank; I could make it, and its furnishings, and its occupants *any way I liked*. Can there be any thrill to match it, this God-like freedom of the mind and spirit?

Soon I knew number 10 Fyffe Street as well as, if not better than, I knew the flat in Balornock. I knew where every light switch was. I knew every crack in every ceiling. I knew much more than I would ever need to put in any book. And this is how it should be.

There are times now when I try to remember my Balornock home and I find I get quite confused. The Farmbank one is still so real to me.

I was able to fill in Catriona's address. The next thing to consider was what age she had to be at the beginning of the story. One had to be careful about the war. For one thing, the chances were the Govan Fair was not held during the war. So many people would be away in the armed forces. It occurred to me at this point that a lot of good emotional stuff could be found in the war years. So it would be a good idea to bring them in later.

This reminds me of a characteristic a novelist has that I haven't yet touched on . It's as if there are two people inside a writer's skin. Flaubert said: "I am, quite literally, two different persons. . . ." (Actually there are lots of people but there are two *main* ones.) For instance, I could be grieving, and grieving sincerely at the death of a loved one. But at the same time, inside me there is the novelist observing, with curious detachment, the event and my every reaction to it; filing everything away to be used if necessary in some future story. Always, all the time, the writer is looking with that cool, curious eye over my shoulder.

I plumped eventually for 1936 when I reckoned Catriona ought to be sixteen. Then came her description. I thought for a while about that and gradually filled in all the details — one detail somehow leading quite smoothly and naturally to another. She had long, fair hair and was small and frail. She was timid and soft-spoken. She was dominated by her mother.

Now, in every character there must be part of yourself. And there is something of me in Catriona. But Catriona is not me. (For one thing, I wasn't as old as sixteen in 1936!) I don't look like her. I didn't get married until I was in my twenties and I had worked at about twenty different jobs before getting married. My first

66

husband was a sailor — four years younger than myself. I was timid, yes. But I was a lot of other things as well. There were times when I could fight back tooth and nail. I had a temper and I had always this strong, persevering spirit.

But as I've stressed before I only needed to take one real characteristic and exaggerate that and I only needed the essence of experience.

A friend of D.H. Lawrence's (Helen Corke) expressed some concern at the way her intimate experiences were being pressed into the service of art. Lawrence replied that he was not falsifying her "truth", he was erecting a work of fiction on a frame of actual experience: "It is my presentation, and therefore necessarily false sometimes to your view. The necessity is not that our two views should coincide but that the work should be a work of art."

While I was filling the first jotter with every detail of Catriona I had to probe into her background. That meant thinking about her parents. So before I knew where I was, my next two characters were being born. Soon I was filling in their details in other notebooks. Soon I knew everything there was to know about Hannah and Rab Munro. As I saw, one things leads to another and when I was filling in details about Rab I had to think about where he would work. I gave this a lot of serious thought. I wanted for the unity and convenience of my story to have a nucleus — a central point where all my characters could meet. From my long apprenticeship in writing I instinctively knew that it would be technically and artistically viable to have the unity of a central core. I felt a need for order. Right from the start too, I felt a need to portray the character of Glasgow.

Gradually the thought of a corner shop wafted into my mind. Impressions and sensations of innumerable corner shops I'd known crowded in on me. And what better than a baker's shop as well as a general store? Yes, yes, with a bakehouse at the back. That way I could have a central scene for action day and night. Then it suddenly came to me — Rab is one of the bakers. The bakers are my characters. The bakers and their families. In fact I would call the book *The Breadmakers*. They could all live in the flats above the bakery. All, that is, except Rab. I couldn't let him live there because if I was going to have Catriona my main character then it was she who must work out her destiny there. It surely would be too inhibiting for her (and me, the author) to have her mother and father living there as well. Anyway, I'd already established that Catriona, Rab and Hannah live in Farmbank.

So how does Catriona get from Farmbank to — I broke off to start yet another notebook, to draw maps of Govan and the imaginary street and bakehouse and shop and all the crush of tenement buildings around it. I eventually called the street Dessie Street. So how does Catriona get to Dessie Street?

But first I had to do research on bakers and bakehouses. I'd never known a baker in my life and I'd never set foot in a bakehouse.

And so my first experience of research began.

# CHAPTER THIRTEEN

IT WAS STRANGE but despite the fact that I could now claim to be a published writer I still hadn't the *belief* that I was a writer. After all, I wasn't a novelist. I hadn't the necessary proof that I was a novelist. That is, I couldn't say that I'd had a book published. So when I went into a baker's shop to ask if I could speak to a baker about his job I felt acutely shy and completely lacking in self-confidence.

I hung away at the back of a crowd of customers until an assistant, spotting me despite my nervous shrinking, called over: "Can I help you?"

My urgent reason for being there stuck in my throat. I felt ashamed and embarrassed. In an effort to appear perfectly normal I asked for half-a-dozen crumpets. While the assistant was putting them into a paper bag I feverishly rehearsed what I had really come to say. But when I found I was being fixed with a gaze of enquiry and encouraged with the words:

"Yes? Was there something else?"

I replied. "Two rhubarb tarts and a small brown loaf."

Eventually, after I'd bought enough cakes and scones and bread to last me all week I blurted out in desperation:

"I'm a writer. I'm writing a book about bakers. Is there a baker here who could help me?" (Is there a baker in the house!)

To my surprise I found the assisant — all the assistants were thrilled. They'd never met a writer before. They dashed into the nether regions of the shop and reappeared after a while with an elderly man who looked as if he'd changed into his best suit and slicked down his hair. He seemed pleased and flattered to have someone interested in him and his job. He, it turned out, was the master baker and the owner of the premises. (What could be better? I immediately decided to have an old master baker in my book and he could own the shop and bakehouse in Dessie Street. In fact, why not make him own the tenement building? That way the bakers in his employ who lived in the flats above would be in "tied houses". I might get a bit of extra drama and conflict out of that.)

I had come prepared with a few basic questions in my notebook. But of course, not knowing anything about the subject I didn't really know what to ask. However, I encouraged the old man to talk freely about his job and I listened with interest. The questions, or the initial lack of them turned out to be no problem. Questions arose out of what he was telling me. As well as being my first experience of doing research, this was also my first lesson in interviewing. I have found people invariably helpful and eager to talk about themselves. The secret is to allow them, to encourage them to talk freely. You should never on these occasions impose your own personality, opinions or views on the conversation. You should never sit in judgement on the other person. You should acquire the art of listening with sympathy and understanding and an open mind — a novelist's mind.

Lionel Trilby said that the novel was the literary form to which the emotions of understanding and forgiveness were indigenous, as if by the definition of the form itself.

Sometimes however, the most difficult part of interviewing someone is to keep a straight face. I well remember one Glasgow woman getting quite carried away about her blackguard of a husband.

"He's a right rotten pig, so he is," she hotly insisted. "I just have nothin' to dae wi' him!"

I couldn't help feeling somewhat bewildered.

"I don't quite understand," I ventured mildly. "I mean, you do have seven children."

She was nonplussed. But only for a moment.

"Aye . . . eh . . . aye . . . but I'm an awful heavy sleeper!"

The old master baker also got quite carried away. I was in his company for hours. There was nothing he didn't tell me about bakers and baking. I even learned that there were particular diseases that bakers were prone to like bronchitis and dermatitis. They tended to go bald as well. I later double-checked on all this from other sources and as I began to get a picture of the lives of these men (remember I'm talking about 1936. That was the time about which I was researching). I also began to get a picture of my "Breadmakers". Soon I had, as well as my old master baker Duncan McNair, his son Melvin who was determined to keep fit and avoid these diseases.

Poor Rab Munro was already afflicted. Hang on! Rab could be off work one time and Melvin could come over to Farmbank with his wages. He would meet Catriona. Now, given the type of person Catriona is, and given the type of person Melvin is — what would happen? And how would Catriona's mother react?

While I'm building all this up, while all these characters are generating emotions (writing is an emotional job because writers deal in nothing but emotions — human emotion starting action and reaction which creates the story), don't forget that I'm still me. I'm still that person who is obsessed with feelings of insecurity, and

70

unworthiness and a terrible need to be loved and wanted for herself. I'm writing from this obsession.

Before I know where I am, without conscious thought, I feel that Catriona is dreaming of one day being safe and secure in a home of her own. If Melvin therefore is a widower and has one of these Dessie Street flats. . . .

Because I've made Catriona timid and lacking in self-confidence, I make Melvin the opposite — an aggressive, conceited bully. Plenty of conflict (and therefore a strong story) should come from that situation when those two characters come together. One must push characters to their limits to get the most drama and feeling however, so I made Melvin not only a widower with a son but a widower who is obsessed with the perfections of his first wife.

Now, I personally know the emotion of this situation but I did not and never have known anyone like Melvin. Having made that quite clear I repeat, I *knew* the emotion. The agony Catriona felt was my agaony. But so was Rab's. And so was Jimmy's and so was Sarah's. In all of these characters I was revealing a kind of nakedness to the world. Dianne Doubtfire said one of the characteristics a novelist needed was courage. I think this is what she meant. You need the courage to be honest in revealing your emotions. Never make the mistake in thinking that this means you can be undisciplined however. You must write within the techniques of the medium. This does not make the emotion less honest. It only conveys it more effectively.

Maupassant said:

> The realist if he is an artist will seek to give us not a banal photographic representation of life but a vision of it that is fuller and more vivid and more compellingly truthful than even reality itself.

I learned a great deal from the writing of *The Breadmakers*. I learned, as I say, how to do research and that one must always check and double check and treble check if possible. Never just accept what one person tells you. It may be *his* truth, but it might not be the whole truth. For instance, apart from the invaluable facts about the art of baking and what machinery was used etc., I got the picture of that old master baker as a benevolent patriarch, loved and respected by all his employees. It really gave me a lovely, cosy picture and I was all set to reflect it in my book. . . . And yet? Instinct, sheer intuition made me insist that I visit the bakehouse later, on my own, without the old gentleman, to put my questions again to the other bakers.

The master baker said there was no need. He had told me everything. There was nothing else anyone could tell me. Still I persisted, making the excuse that I needed to see the bakehouse during the night (the old master baker only worked days now) to soak up the different atmosphere. Eventually I got my way and one night when everyone else was sleeping, I set off through the dark streets to the bakehouse. That journey was invaluable for a start. Glasgow is a different world in the middle of the night. The bakehouse was a different place in the middle of the night. The bakers were different people in the middle of the night. While I sat eating hot, freshly baked rolls oozing with butter and drinking tea from a mug, I listened sympathetically to them. I discovered that far from being a benevolent old gentleman their boss, as far as they were concerned, was not only a mean, foul-mouthed old tyrant but a right randy old bugger as well.

I hadn't at this early stage found that excellent book by Ann Hoffman called *Research*. In that book there is everything you need to know about researching. But when I was working on *The Breadmakers* I was on my own and playing everything by ear. Well, I say on my own but in actual fact I soon found the Mitchell Reference Library in Glasgow and the librarians there, especially those in the Glasgow Room, of invaluable assistance to me. No question or problem I presented them with proved too difficult to crack, no piece of information too elusive to track down. I don't mean that libraries do your research for you. You've no right to expect that. Nine times out of ten, however, they can produce a book or books or old newspapers or manuscripts which you can search through and find a treasure trove of helpful material you never dreamed existed. And, as I keep repeating, one thing leads to another.

Years after *The Breadmakers*, I was asked by my publishers to write a historical novel. I'll tell you a little about that book at this stage because it is a good example of what I mean by this chain reaction and how research helps you find characters and build plots. I didn't know anything about historical novels. I'd never read one since I was in my teens. I hadn't a clue how to write one. But it had become my policy as far as writing was concerned to say yes, when I was asked to do something, then worry about it afterwards. The historical book was one big worry, I can tell you. I didn't want to write it. But I needed the money.

"Try to make it something with an American connection," was the only help I got from the publisher.

The worst of it was, as well as not knowing anything about historical novels, I didn't know anything about history!

I thought and thought and worried and worried. Gradually I

became aware of a hazy recollection of having heard somewhere, something about Glasgow Tobacco Lords. Tobacco? Maybe that had some connection with America? Off I went to the Mitchell Library.

"I'm thinking of writing a book about the Glasgow Tobacco Lords," I told the librarians in the special room that houses the Glasgow Collection. "Could you help me?"

They could.

I settled down with my notebook at one of the tables and was soon lost to sight among mountains of books. The tobacco lords were wealthy merchants of Glasgow. There was indeed a connection with America, I discovered — a very lucrative trade in tobacco with Virginia. The trade was at its peak, I read, in 1745. That rang a bell! 1745? There was something else going on in that year, was there not?

Who would have thought it! At exactly this time Bonny Prince Charlie was hell-bent on invading England. To my great interest I discovered that the Glasgow tobacco lords — who were also the magistrates who ran Glasgow — were against Charlie and had raised a body of men called the Glasgow Sharpshooters to fight alongside the English against the Scottish prince. Plenty of conflict there then. I was delighted. Already I had the makings of "a cracking good tale". But wait — even better was to come: the prince's followers wanted to burn Glasgow to the ground and the highland army were outside Glasgow threatening to do just that. I could imagine the scene. I could feel the apprehension of all the Glasgow people. Eventually a bargain was struck. A huge sum of money was paid to the prince by the merchants who also agreed to kit out the whole highland army. Meantime the army rode and marched into the city to billet itself on the people.

All I needed to do was to begin a few "character notebooks" as I'd done with *The Breadmakers* but this time greatly helped by reading about the actual characters — rich and poor — who lived in and around the city at the time. All I had to do to kick off my story was to ask myself what each character would feel and how they would react to enemy soldiers (there were also French and Irish mercenaries with the highland army) invading their city and their houses.

I discovered, too, the knack of blending into my fiction narrative, real-life characters and incidents gleaned from books about old worthies, and newspaper reports of happenings and biographies of men and women of the period. (Journals and diaries are also great sources of material.)

I came across some hilarious anecdotes which I incorporated

73

into my story — like the funeral where everyone got so drunk, it wasn't until they reached the graveside that they discovered they'd forgotten the body.

I enjoyed writing my eighteenth-century historical trilogy in the end. Yes, like *The Breadmakers* it turned out to be, not one book but three.

Don't ever say you can't think of anything to write about! There's stories by the million just waiting to be told.

# CHAPTER FOURTEEN

I MADE MISTAKES with *The Breadmakers*. I used some historical facts in it and instead of weaving them into the fabric of the story I tended to start a chapter with a lead in of historical information. For instance, I begin Chapter Two with several paragraphs telling of when and how the Govan Fair originated. Interesting stuff but all the same if I were writing that chapter today I think I, the author, would keep out of it and the information would be conveyed through a conversation between a couple of the story characters or through the thoughts of one of the characters.

There are two big dangers with research. One, you get too interested in researching *per se* and you delay getting down to the creative writing. Two, you discover so much fascinating information you feel compelled to share it all with your readers. You are eager to give them as much of your treasure trove of facts as possible. It must be remembered however, that once you start to write you are not a researcher or a historian or a teacher. You are a storyteller. Right away your first duty is to get inside the skins of your characters and the only information that should go into your book is what your *characters* would need to know, or see, or be interested in, in the particular place and the particular time in which they are living and working out their destinies.

I had meant *The Breadmakers* to cover about eight years or so in the lives of my characters. That way I'd get the war in. However, once I'd written what I thought was an average booklength manuscript I found only a year had passed. That's why I had to press on and write a second book, *A Baby Might Be Crying*. I wrote it while *The Breadmakers* was bouncing back and forward between Glasgow and London with depressing regularity.

New characters kept popping up with new storylines until I was interweaving so many I had to keep myself surrounded by notebooks in which I kept track of everyone's age, their relationship to each other and where they all were and why. I suppose this is where John Braine's "full-scale engineering in words" comes in. The age business is especially tricky and complicated. You've got to know all along the line what age every character is and what ages their children are in relation to other children and to fictitious events that are going on and to real-life happenings of the time.

I had to press on and write a third book in which to work everything out to a satisfactory conclusion. I called it *A Sort of Peace* and

I wrote it while *The Breadmakers* and *A Baby Might Be Crying* were collecting rejection slips and costing me a fortune in postage.

Mind you, I wept. Oh, how I wept. But it wasn't so much (if at all) over the rejection slips. It was the sheer exhausting hard work of it all. Talk about blood, sweat and tears! *A Baby Might Be Crying* was the killer. I'd given myself two main and serious challenges in this book. First, I'd introduced a new character called Alec Jackson into whose mind I went. Secondly, I bring in the war, part of which is seen through Alec's eyes.

It wasn't the first time I'd gone into a male character's mind, of course. I had done this with Jimmy and Rab in *The Breadmakers*. For a woman writer this is always a difficult and challenging thing to do and I'm not saying I found it easy with the characters in *The Breadmakers*. However, the models that I had used for Rab and Jimmy had been my father and my brother. I had taken certain characteristics that I had observed in them over a long period and from these closely observed characteristics I had created my fictitious males.

Alec Jackson was something else. I'd modelled him on a relation as well but this relation was a man I'd only met briefly a very few times since my childhood. all I had to go on was a memory of his laughing, sexy eyes and the habit he had of taking a naughty double meaning out of everything anybody said. I had a feeling that he was a bit of a rascal but attractive with it. Likeable too. From this vague feeling I created Alec Jackson and I believe the reason he comes to life more vividly than Rab or Jimmy as a person in his own right is because I remembered my father and brother too well.

André Gide had a similar experience. In his logbook of *The Coiners* he wrote:

> If I spoiled the portrait of old La Pérouse it was because I clung too closely to reality; I neither knew nor was able to lose sight of my model. The narrative of that first visit will have to be done over. La Pérouse will not come to life nor shall I really visualize him until he completely displaces his original. Nothing so far has given me so much trouble. The difficult thing is inventing when you are encumbered by memory. . . .

Then, as I say, there was the war and Alec had to go to the war and I had to be there with him — yea, even unto the beaches of Dunkirk!

Oh, dear, oh, dear, I get a headache even now when I think of my struggles over that story. In the first place I must have read at least a dozen books by men of all ranks who had actually been to

Dunkirk. I had also read the descriptions and feelings of the people who took the armada of small boats to the beaches. I had to find and speak to people who had been there.

And all the time I was realizing more and more how I loathed and detested war and the terrible suffering it caused. This brings me to an important point. I did not, before I started that book, have any conscious commitment.

Irving Wallace said:

> I don't think that every writer must be committed. Of course, one is always committed — from the social point of view and in one's current life. But as a writer, it's not absolutely necessary. A writer is what he is; and I think he should write what he feels like writing and do it the best he can. I live in a world of ideas, and I want to propagate my ideas.
>
> However, experience shows that it is not ideas that permit a work to survive but characters. Ideas change but man remains. I believe that a novel of commitment can be literature, but if so, the reason is the depth of its characterizations. But one simply can't think of that as he writes. You simply don't think of such things: you simply write.

By the time Alec was on a ship on his way to Dunkirk, I knew him. I knew how he would view the whole business. I simply wrote what Alec saw.

Another character in that book was Sammy, a conscientious objector. Again, I didn't write out of some pre-planned commitment. I didn't create Sammy as my anti-war mouthpiece. Sammy became a CO because of his hatred for his father who was a military man and a tyrant. I based Sammy's father on my paternal grandfather. I tell you something I've just this minute realized. I didn't know at the time why I called my character Sammy. It was only just now, when I mentioned that I'd based Sammy's father on my paternal grandfather, that I realized I had called him the same name as my father. Not that my father was ever a CO. In fact he ran away to the army when he was, I think, only thirteen or fourteen. And no wonder he ran away to the army. (They sent him back when they discovered he was under age.) and then left home and went into digs when he was fifteen or sixteen. His father was a real shocker! With a father like that you just had to make some sort of protest. Or go under.

Once I had a CO on my hands (I was going into his mind too; I think I must be a masochist), I had to find out all about COs and how they were treated. That certainly gave me more drama and plot material. I had a whole scene at a tribunal, for instance, which was perfectly authentic. There was also the set-up in the detention unit of Maryhill Barracks which I got from men who'd been imprisoned there. Another scene in that book takes place in the barracks and involves a fight between Sammy and two very tough soldiers. I remember sweating over the writing of this in my efforts to get it realistic. I thought I'd done a pretty good job but — as usual — I decided to check just to make sure. I gave it to one of my sons to read, warning him as I did so:

"Don't be shocked, son. It's rough and there's some bad words in it."

He read it then fell about laughing.

"Call all that fisticuffs tough? For goodness' sake, Mum. Get the boot in!"

I immediately rewrote the whole scene in an entirely different manner and when my son read it again he said it was now perfectly believable.

Catriona — now married to Melvin — is also in this book and she is involved in the air-raids. I drew on my memories of the raids on Glasgow and how we used to all troop downstairs every night (we lived in the top flat at the time) and take shelter in Mrs McWhirter's windowless lobby. She was our neighbour who lived in the bottom flat. I remember my mother wasn't very popular on one occasion when she gazed heavenwards in the direction of the German bombers and announced:

"God help them. They're some poor mothers' sons!"

In *A Baby Might Be Crying* everyone takes shelter in the windowless lobby that separated the bakehouse at the back from the shop at the front. In the book something terrible happens and people get killed. In real life the worst that happened in Mrs McWhirter's was one night, Mr Kirby, another neighbour had gone to the door to peep nervously out, suddenly staggered back howling among us. We thought a bullet or a piece of flying shrapnel had got him but it turned out somebody had shut the door on his thumb.

It can be a sore thing that.

By the time I had finished *A Baby Might Be Crying* I had said something important — at least it was important to me — that I had not set out to say at the beginning. It's an odd fact that artists achieve the effect of a message usually only when they don't intend it. Their sermon is most efficacious if they have no notion they are preaching one. They are like the bee who produces wax for her own purposes, unaware that folk will think up different uses for it.

Critics and academics read much into the work of writers and expound on what was meant when in fact the writers didn't know what they meant themselves, or they meant something quite different and far less complicated. (Although, of course, there are some writers who muddy their own waters to appear more deep.)

Graham Greene when questioned about symbolism in one of his books replied: "But there is no deep symbolism — or if there is, it's not my job to find it. Critics and university professors rejoice in the *sous-texte* these days. The study of fiction has become less the study of the narrative art than a search for arcane meanings. . . . I try to be a straight writer."

Steinbeck said: "We work in our own darkness a great deal with little real knowledge of what we are doing. I think I know better what I'm doing than most writers but it still isn't much."

Once asked the meaning of certain lines, Browning replied: "When I wrote these lines, God and Browning knew what they meant. Now only God knows!"

When T.S. Elliot was asked what he meant when he wrote, "Three white leopards sat under a Juniper tree," he answered: "Three white leopards sat under a Juniper tree!"

# CHAPTER FIFTEEN

BY THIS TIME my dearly loved brother Audley had died and it is to his memory that I dedicated *The Breadmakers*. My mother, his young wife and I sat with him hour after hour holding his hand, listening to his terrible breathing as, even in his unconscious state, he fought to cling on to life.

The day before when I visited him in the hospital, I believe he knew not only that he'd taken a relapse but that he was going to die. He looked at me with tragic, fear-filled eyes and said:

"I was up on Christmas day, Margaret. I was nearly getting out. I sang 'Bye Bye Blackbird' at the party."

I can never hear that song without feeling anguished.

When I was leaving the ward that afternoon (he was alone in a small room and I wish he hadn't been alone), my mother stopped me and said:

"Kiss him."

And I did.

Then going along the corridor she told me:

"He's not going to get better." I still see her face, the depth of her suffering giving it a lovely dignity. Why did I speak harshly to her in reply? I said not to talk nonsense and that Audley was going to be all right. I didn't mean to sound curt or cruel. I suppose it was just that I couldn't bear to face the truth. I didn't have the courage. She had though.

I never saw him conscious again. At evening visiting time his eyes were closed and the room was filled with the nightmare noise of his breathing.

My mother and father are dead now but, much as I loved them, I never wept so brokenheartedly for either of them as I did for my brother. And every night alone in bed (my husband drove his taxi at night) I frantically sobbed out prayers, pleading with God to understand how Audley had been an atheist and to forgive him. (He had asked that there would be no ministers at his funeral.)

I wonder myself why Audley was an atheist. My father was an atheist. Was that the reason? Did Audley love and admire him more than we knew? Or was it a kind of survival kit against my mother's overwhelming love for him? She was a strong Christian (the United Free Church). It must have been difficult for a boy to retain his masculinity in his circumstances. And he certainly did retain his masculinity and his independence. Because of his ill-health my mother tended to be over-anxious about him and tried to stop him taking any exercise or any part in sports. Yet despite her undermining anxieties and warnings of the awful consequences he went ahead and played tennis and cricket. He never argued with her. As far as I remember he was always kind and patient and loving towards her. Nevertheless he stuck to his guns.

Audley daren't give up or give in. Maybe that's why when he was in hospital with that last illness he told his wife not to let my mother in to see hin. Eventually, of course, she had to get in when his condition worsened. I think I understand how he felt about my mother. I know he loved her. But love can make you so vulnerable, can't it? He was only trying to be brave.

He was so clever and talented. He had to leave school early because of the rheumatic fever but he had educated himself. And he taught himself to play the piano. (That's why I had Jimmy in *The Breadmakers* play the piano.) This must have been another example of his independent spirit because surely my mother would have been only too eager to teach him if he'd given her the chance? I have no recollection of ever seeing my mother with my brother at the piano. But oh how I do remember him with his dark curly head bent over the keyboard, his pale face tense with concentration as he forced his rheumaticky fingers to move. He used to pencil above each note on a piece of music c, d, e, f or whatever he had discovered it was. Then with excruciating patience and perseverance he'd find the notes on the piano and play them. He'd play the first bar of the music that way, over and over and over again until he'd got it perfect. Only then would he move on to the next bar and so on through the whole piece. It was never a simple modern piece either. I remember Rachmaninov's Prelude for instance being repeated and repeated with desperate loving care. Until my father would rage into the room shouting:

"Stop that infernal racket, you fool, before I go stark raving mad!"

When my brother was small no one could have been more loving and patient with him than my father. Audley adored him and right to the end, no matter what my father did or didn't do, Audley remained hotly loyal to him. That was why it was so tragic that in latter years my father acted as if he violently hated Audley. (Not all the time, of course, but violent emotion began to explode to the surface more and more often.)

Who's to blame? Who starts what? And why? I don't know. All I'm sure of is that a novelist should at least try to understand, should try to work out motivation not blame.

After Audley's death I never saw my mother shed a tear. But my father became distracted and went around the house whimpering

Audley's name. And within a matter of weeks he had collapsed with a heart attack. He survived that first attack and my mother said to him:

"Why should you be alive and my son dead? Why couldn't it have been you?"

She must have been tormented by a terrible burden of bitterness as well as grief. But I can see her yet at the funeral tea held in her front room after everyone had returned from my brother's cremation.

The room was crowded and her handsome, straight-backed figure moved briskly about seeing to everyone's needs. The way she was behaving in her usual cheery hospitable manner no one would have guessed that the gathering was in any way different from the much-enjoyed parties she was in the habit of giving. She even told some of her funny anecdotes and had everyone laughing.

I think, looking back, the time I'm talking about must surely have been the worst period of my life. And yet I suppose it was as much an apprenticeship for the job of novelist as all the practice in writing I'd done. Everything was torn and anguished and confused. From the time of my brother's death I felt I was watching the destruction of my father. My mother never let him be. Even as she and I sat either side of his hospital bed her bitter tongue continuously cut him to pieces and he, with his temper, never failed to be roused into retaliation. It tortured me to see him, eyes protruding with distress, breathlessly fighting back. I could do nothing to stop it. I tried but only made things worse.

The danger of interfering is that no one knows the whole truth about a relationship, not even one of the family and the person trying to help only adds more fuel to the fire.

My father was a big powerful man. He survived that heart attack but he was never the same again. He became terribly anxious about money and the future. He got into panics too easily. Even if he couldn't find his spectacles he panicked. My mother said it was sheer lack of control like his wicked bad temper.

They fought tooth and nail until the day he died. He had been along the road at the local pub for a drink. When he returned he couldn't find his Post Office savings book which he thought he'd had in his pocket. He got into one of his panics and I can just imagine how, at the same time, my mother's tongue would be flaying him. He left to go back along the road to look for his savings book. But, for no apparent reason, he returned within a couple of minutes and, as my mother told me later:

"He just stood in the doorway and looked at me. And I said, 'Well? What are you standing there for?' Then, without answering, he turned and went away again."

On reaching the pub he collapsed, blood gushing from his mouth and was dead before the ambulance arrived.

Afterwards my mother wept and said to me: "Oh, the pity of it!"

I never saw her weep again but later when I was in a shop with her helping to buy clothes for the funeral she suddenly looked at me in anguish and said:

"Was I not nice to him, Margaret?"

I immediately reassured her that of course she had been nice to him and he had always thought the world of her. As indeed he had.

"Your mammy's a wonderful woman," he used to say.

She seemed to be reassured and in the weeks and months and years that followed I've listened in absolute astonishment as she's related stories to friends about "my Sam" and what a wonderful husband he'd been and what a beautiful and happy relationship they'd had.

"Never once did a cross word pass between us," I've heard her say.

She also used to tell everyone that "poor Sam" had "dropped in the street". Alone with me however, she'd say, "Fancy him dying in a pub!" As if perverse to the last, he'd done it just to spite her.

My father always carried the key of the coal-celler about in his pocket. In their last house there was a coal-cellar out on the landing next to the front door. They didn't need it for coal because in that house they had an electric fire but my father used the cellar in which to experiment with home-made wines. My mother hated "the demon drink" and so never went near the place

After my father died I was given the task of clearing out his things. Eventually I got round to tackling the coal-cellar. I unlocked the door. Inside, there was no wine. There were hundreds of bars of soap, and quarter-pound packets of Co-op tea, and tins of corned beef, and mountains of baked beans and packets of my mother's favourite "pink pudding".

Here was my father's fearful insecurity, his desperate, secret efforts to provide the necessities of life for my mother and himself in their old age.

My mother never worried about tomorrow.

"Tomorrow will take care of itself," she used to say. "God will provide."

But my father was an atheist.

# CHAPTER SIXTEEN

YOU NEVER really know about everyone though, do you? That's why I say a writer should never make snap judgements, should never take people at face value. My father used to glower at my mother and insist he was an atheist. If she put the wireless on at a church service he would switch it off. She would switch it on again. And he would switch it off again. It was one of their battlegrounds. The switch on, switch off usually came at the climax of one of their arguments. My mother's dogmatic illogicality drove him out of his wits.

She was the same with everybody. I remember on one occasion she was arguing with my son Kenneth. She had stated quite categorically that it was violence in books that caused violence in people. Kenneth said what about jungle tribes who could be very violent, even cannibalistic, without ever reading any books. Her reply was a triumphant: "Aye, but the rascals *would* read them if they got the chance!"

My father when alone with me preferred to use the term agnostic to describe himself. Yet often I even wondered about that. He never missed hearing, and watching on television, the Pope giving his yearly message. He seemed to genuinely enjoy and appreciate the occasion, even find comfort in it. I think, too, all the colour and pageantry fired his vivid imagination. I believe my father was a very emotional man. Although I don't think he would have liked anyone to say so. He prided himself on being able to keep a cool head in an argument. He used to say to me:

"Never allow an argument to sink to a personal level."

In his bookcase, as well as his Left Book Club books there were titles like *How To Argue and Win* and *The Art of Logical Thought*. No doubt they had stood him in good stead in his early days when he'd been the only working-class man on the West Lothian Education Committee but with my mother they were worse than useless. No matter what the topic happened to be and no matter how my father struggled to stick to the point, he was always defeated by my mother's special brand of illogicality.

They would be debating the Spanish Civil War for instance and she would say:

"You're a fine one to talk — you that spent three pounds on drink last week. The publican's wife will have a fur coat all right!"

He did worse things than take a few drinks. I remember one

terrible time my mother had left him for some reason or other. She was always leaving him as a punishment and while she was away she would write in her dashing scribble a long, confusingly unpunctuated letter with a liberal sprinkling of capital letters whenever and wherever it took her fancy, cataloguing his sins and informing him what he must do or must not do in order to get her back.

In reply she would receive a single page of such tiny, neat, beautifully formed words it was truly a work of art. It took the form of an apology and always began, "Dear Chrissie," and ended: "Yours sincerely, Samuel Thomson."

"Would you look at that?" my mother used to say, showing me the letter. "We've been married for donkeys' years and he still puts 'Samuel Thomson'. Did you ever hear of such an awkward man in all your life? I'll Samuel Thomson him!"

There was usually a present waiting for her when she did return. I remember once a lovely half-set of china that my father had set out ready for her in all its splendour on the living-room table.

But the time which sticks in my memory was when my mother returned to find he'd sold her piano. It must have been one of the times when I had been left behind, because I was standing in the doorway of the front room when she came in. I must have been quite small because I had no idea what had been happening or why. I looked up at my mother and saw her stunned face. Panic smacked across her eyes before she could stiffen against it. It was the first time I'd seen her look vulnerable. It had always seemed to me that she was on the winning side.

I don't know why my father did it. I was too young to know. Maybe he desperately needed the money and had no choice. Maybe there was some reason that he couldn't help. I hope so, because if he did it simply as a means of getting the better of my mother, it was horribly cruel.

But, despite the fact that she reeled under the blow and must have suffered an agony of loss, she was far from allowing anyone to get the better of her. She played a neighbour's piano instead. She had a defiant ripple at everyone's piano. Until eventually, God alone knows how, she got another piano herself.

It never occurred to my father that all he ever succeeded in doing was to give her more ammunition to fire against him. Not that he needed to do this after my brother died. Neither he nor my mother were ever the same again.

My mother took a dislike to the house they were living in in Broomknowes Road. It was an unlucky house, she insisted. She came to hate it as if it had killed my brother and no doubt it had, even although he hadn't slept in it for over a decade. They moved house and then she said she could never feel at home in the new place. She started hankering after a house near Audley's widow. She clung to my brother's widow as if somehow in her there was still a part of him.

I explored this mother-in-law/daughter-in-law relationship in the third book of my trilogy which also dealt with the last part of the war and the post-war period and was called *A Sort of Peace*.

I dealt with the real emotion but not the real people. Julie, a shopgirl from the Gorbals and her RAF officer husband had nothing in common with my sister-in-law who belonged to Balornock and my brother who would never have been physically fit for any kind of military service. Nobody could be less like my mother than Mrs Muriel Vincent, Julie's mother-in-law in the book.

By the time I came to that third book I had already set characters in the north side of Glasgow and in the south of the city but I hadn't yet characterized the east side and the west side. I say characterized because I was in fact trying to capture the character of Glasgow as well as its people. So, I thought to myself — this time I must set one of my main characters in the east side of the city and another main character in the west end.

I started wandering around the west end. At that time I knew nothing about that part of the city. In my wanderings I happened across a lovely, leafy crescent that looked down on to the back of the Botanic Gardens. This was the very place, I decided. Before long, as I strolled back and forth along the crescent I had made up my mind that Catriona and Melvin would move here too. (In the last book they had been made homeless.) I set them in one of the terrace houses at one end. There were red sandstone flats at the other end and my new west-end characters could live there.

I was just trying to make up my mind about these new characters and visualize them when out of one of the red sandstone buildings emerged a petite genteel lady. She asked me if there was anything she could do to help — was I lost or something? I hadn't realized how odd I must have looked walking from one end of the crescent to the other and back again about a hundred and one times.

I explained that I was a writer and I had decided that one of my characters should live in one of these flats and although I couldn't know what the flats were like inside I had to at least familiarize myself with the outside of the place. I had to know what someone living here would know about the surroundings.

She was entranced. But of course I must know all about the *inside* of the flats as well. All I needed to do was follow her upstairs

86

and wander about inside her flat. What's more, she would make me a cup of tea while I was doing it. Glasgow people really are exceptionally kind.

It was such a help to me to get the proper layout, and the feel of that house and to have the lovely green view from the window pointed out to me. It also helped in other ways to meet this dear wee lady because she triggered off a picture of petite and ladylike Mrs Muriel Vincent in my head,.

If Mrs Muriel Vincent had to live in the west end however, that meant young Julie had to come from the east end. Next day I began exploring around the maze of tenements that made up Bridgeton, Calton and the Gorbals. They were knocking the Gorbals down and it occurred to me that it might be a good idea to make a human as well as geographical record of the old place before everyone and everything disappeared. So the Gorbals it was!

When I eventually finished writing that book and therefore the trilogy of books, can you imagine how I felt? It seemed incredible to me at the time that I'd actually managed to overcome all the problems the writing of such a long work entailed. I had a wonderful sense of achievement (and relief). But most important of all was the thrill of having made a whole new world and peopled it with characters of my own creation.

This thrill, this glorious sense of achievement, was worth every tear shed during the writing, every headache, even every disappointment afterwards. (Now I had three books bouncing back and forwards between Glasgow and London.) There's something else too, something almost mystical. I used to listen to lectures by published novelists and they'd tell how one of the characters in their books "took off on her own" or "acquired a life of his own" or "took over and became a person in his or her own right — quite apart from me, the author".

What airy-fairy nonsense is this? I used to ask myself. Who are they trying to kid?

Yet, believe it or not, by the time I had finished *The Breadmakers* trilogy — indeed by the time I'd finished the first book of the trilogy — I knew what these authors meant. They had been telling the exact truth.

When I started writing *The Breadmakers* I had no jotter written up for Sarah and when she first appeared in the book I meant her to be no more than the wife of one of the bakers — a very minor character. I intended Catriona to be the one with whom the readers identified and had most sympathy for. Despite my intention, however, Sarah began to take over. That to me seemed strange enough but what I found quite frightening, almost creepy, was when at one point I was sitting at my desk writing and suddenly, unbidden, out of a blank mind — or was it out of my subconscious? — I heard Sarah say something that was perfectly in character with her but something that was quite alien to me. And I saw her. She shuffled across my mind's eye — as clear — as clear — I cannot tell you. My stomach flips nervously over even yet.

One reviewer said of *The Breadmakers:*

". . . Although the plot holds our interest all the way, the characters reveal the real talent of this author. She cares passionately for people. And it shows. Her portrait of Sarah, the poor, pain-ridden housewife who isn't responsible for her actions is one of the best things in the book."

# CHAPTER SEVENTEEN

AT ONE POINT all three books came back to me at once from different publishers. I then made one big parcel of the three of them and posted it to a publisher I hadn't yet tried.

They kept the trilogy for nine months. During that time I kept my hand in by writing two more novels. One was called *The Prisoner* and was set in wealthy Bearsden. Or at least mostly set in Bearsden. Three of the characters lived in working-class Maryhill. In quite a few ways this book was different from my *Breadmakers* trilogy. In the first place, it is comparatively short and it hasn't any humour — or very little compared with my other books. Somehow I just couldn't see the main character Celia's predicament as a bundle of laughs, no matter what way I looked at it.

In retrospect, the problems that arose while I was writing that book are hilarious. But, believe me, they were absolutely ghastly at the time and did nothing to enhance my social standing and personality rating in douce and respectable Bearsden. I recall one terrible mix-up when I had to prepare and deliver a speech to a very posh and dignified dinner-gathering which included the Lord Provost, local school teachers and other professional people including a couple of ministers of religion.

Now, for anyone who hasn't read *The Prisoner,* it's about a very frustrated woman who thinks about nothing but sex all the time. And the thing is, as I've said before, a writer has to get under the skin of her characters and really feel as they feel. Well, I wasn't aware of it at the time but when I started to read my speech I soon realized to my horror that it was getting sexier and sexier. *It was sex- obsessed.* I was even beginning to tell dirty jokes! I floundered on, desperately trying to censor myself as I went along. But, at one never-to-be-forgotten moment, I found myself staring eyeball to eyeball at a man of the cloth and out of my mouth were coming the awful words:

"Did you hear about the minister who discovered that one of his flock was a prostitute? He was terribly shocked and upset about this and the very next day he sought out the fallen sheep and said to her — 'Oh, daughter, I prayed for you last night.' And she said, 'Och, you didn't need to do that. I'm on the phone!'"

Nobody laughed. Except the Lord Provost who was immediately silenced by his wife. I was glad when I finished that book. It took a lot out of me.

The next one was triggered off by a news item in the morning paper. It immediately involved both my emotions and my curiosity. It was remarking on the commendable fact of the absence of any colour prejudice in Glasgow but went on to say that it might be a different situation once immigrant families started moving out to the middle-class suburbs. I wondered what might happen if a Pakistani family tried to settle in Bearsden. Once you begin to ask yourself "What if?" and "How would?" and "Why?" — you've started the story-building process.

By this time I knew the value (and the necessity) of research, so I decided that before I could put pen to paper I'd have to find out about Pakistanis. I'd have to get to know them.

Now, I'd never met, never spoken to one coloured person in my life. Normally I found it easy to get to know people. People usually seem to sense that I'm genuinely and sympathetically interested in them. Complete strangers have told me their life stories while we've stood together in a queue waiting for a bus. People have confided their most intimate troubles to me in launderettes and in trains.

Initially all that's usually necessary is a friendly smile or opening remark. But Pakistanis always seemed so dour and withdrawn, especially the women. They seemed to purposely shut you out and not want anything to do with anyone except their own kind. Nothing daunted however, I wrote to one of the Glasgow councillors who is a Pakistani. I explained about my book and my need to get to know a Pakistani family and could he help me to meet one? I managed to get an interview with this councillor who was in fact most helpful. He explained that there would be language difficulties, not to mention different customs. He thought the best idea was for me to get in touch with a Miss Reekie who could speak Urdu and who acted as a kind of liaison for the immigrant community.

I was eventually invited to Miss Reekie's flat one Sunday afternoon. What a fascinating afternoon that turned out to be. Her front room was crowded with not only Pakistani men, women and children; a few West Indians and Chinamen had come along for good measure. The place was so packed, half of us had to sit on the floor. The talk was so loud and, to a Scotswoman like myself who had never been used to any foreign accent worse than English, it was most terribly confusing. I'm sure my ears must have grown that day, I was straining and stretching them so much. It wouldn't have been so bad if one Chinaman hadn't kept playing the flute.

At one point I was jammed on a sofa between him and a plump Pakistani lady called Mrs Mogul who was knitting furiously and talking even more furiously about a journey she and her husband had recently made to England. While in that country she had gone into a shop and the shopkeeper had asked "Where do you come from?"

Mrs Mogul had proudly replied: "I come from Glasgow, Scotland."

"What?" sneered the shopkeeper. "That dump!"

"You no like Scotland?" Mrs Mogul was outraged even by the memory of the occasion. "'I no like England!' I told him!"

She flung her knitting down and went, muttering, to help Miss Reekie with the tea.

I was joined by a pretty Pakistani girl called Shafiga. But before we could get talking, Miss Reekie herded a family of five little Pakistani boys into the room and announced that they were going to give a song. They were lined up and, after a few proddings from Miss Reekie and everyone else who came within prodding distance, they burst into a charming, if somewhat squeaky rendering of "Jesus loves me, this I know, for the Bible tells me so. . . ."

Eventually the Chinaman put down his flute so that he could drink his tea and I got chatting to Shafiga. She said she would be very pleased to help me with my research. She invited me to visit her home as often as I wished and assured me that her father and all her family would help too. As a result, a few days later I was making my way somewhat nervously along one of the poorer streets of the city. It was a dark, winter's night and all I could see around me in the shadows of closes and at street corners were dark-skinned men who were talking in a strange tongue. I had my tape-recorder (I used it for interviews) slung over my shoulder and I clutched at it as if for support. I needn't have been afraid, however. I was safer in that street among the Pakistani men than among anyone else, anywhere else in Glasgow. Pakistanis have a respect for women and for the safeguarding of a woman's good character. My friends told me they had a saying: "If money is lost, nothing is lost. If health is lost, something is lost. But if character is lost, everything is lost."

Shafiga's father had been a trained dispenser in Pakistan and had been called "Hakim" or "Doctor" and treated with much respect. Over here, however, his qualifications were no use and he was too old to start a new training. Eventually the only job he could get was as a lamplighter.

"Margaret," he said to me, "this is no good for an old man. I have the sore knees with up down, up down so many stairs. My legs they feel they are walking all the way to Pakistan and back!"

I learned so much from these people and I owe them a great

debt of gratitude. I was jolted into a new awareness and under-standing. Things I'd taken for granted, or never thought about, had to be thought about and looked at in a new light. Even small things, like when one of the sisters, Nargus, the youngest, a teen-ager still at school told me excitedly that she was wearing new trousers.

"Look, Margaret! New trousers!" She cried, clapping her hands. She was in a seventh heaven of rapture and I couldn't see why. They were nice enough trousers but all the same. . . .

"Bell bottoms!" she squealed. "Bell bottoms, Margaret!"

It was only then that it occurred to me why this was such an exciting and unusual event to her. All her life until then she had been forced to wear the tight at the ankle Eastern trousers. Bell-bottoms were Western dress. She had made a break with tradition, taken an exciting step into a new world. Suddenly I understood how she felt. I began to understand how these women felt in lots of other ways. Especially the older women. I began to see how frightening and shocking our Western way of life can seem to them. It is part of their religion, for instance, that a woman should be modestly covered from head to toe. When my Pakistani women friends visited me at first they used to hastily cover their heads with their scarves if my husband entered the room. They also rose to give him a seat which was somewhat off-putting for him. When he offered to give them a lift home they stared at him in nervous silence until I, sensing it wasn't the done thing for them to be alone with a strange man, offered to go too.

The majority of older women in Pakistan are illiterate. Also most of them, for all their lives before coming here, were hidden in the burkah, a heavy tent-like garment with just a tiny grating-type window for the eyes to peer out. Think yourself into a burkah for a minute. Firstly, nobody can see you. You don't need to have any expression on your face at all. There's no need even to acquire the habit of smiling. Your face will be relaxed and completely untutored in the lively, varied, sophisticated range of expressions that have become second nature to us in the West. Imagine having that protective covering suddenly ripped off, and in a strange land where everyone is a different colour and speaks a different language, and has strange customs and philosophies.

The first difficulty I had to struggle with was the language. I became particularly friendly with Parveen, the married daughter, whose husband Ibrahim worked on the buses. Parveen had been taught English at the school she had been educated at in Pakistan and she spoke very good English — as did they all, except "mummy" who couldn't speak any. Even with Parveen, though, the accent — part Glasgow, part Pakistan — made it very confusing. We had all sorts of misunderstandings and mix-ups. Like when I arrived on a visit and I thought Parveen said:

"Will you have coffee or tea?"

"I'll have tea, thank you!" I promptly replied.

But Parveen had actually said: "Take off your coat, please."

I wondered at her surprised and bewildered expression. Then, when the truth dawned on me, I was terribly embarrassed.

"You must think I'm awfully cheeky," I said, apologising.

"No, no, you are not cheeky," she hastened to assure me. "You have tea or cofee or curry or chapattis or anything in our house. You are like family. We have a love with you!"

The really difficult thing to grasp and to practise is not the language, however. It is the switching over to see everything from their viewpoint. The only way I can explain this is to give another example.

While talking to Shafiga I discovered that Muslim parents arrange marriages for both their sons and their daughters and there is no such thing as having boyfriends or girlfriends or courting before mariage. I thought it was the natural thing to do to show sympathy when discussing this with Shafiga.

"That's terrible!" I said indignantly. "You should be free to choose your own husband. It should be your choice!"

To my surprise, she answered with matching surprise.

"But why? Can it be that I am wiser and know more about these things than my mother and father? No, no, I trust my parents to do what is best for me. They love me you see."

"But," I persisted, "what if the marriage doesn't work out? What if you are incompatible?"

Shafiga replied, "Oh, there are very few divorces in our country. Pakistani women are very reasonable. If we do something which does not please our husbands, our husbands only need to tell us — and we change!"

Other Pakistani women joined in our conversation and were curious to know how we in the West met our marriage partners. Do you know, I found that a kind of difficult thing to explain.

"Oh, er . . . at parties, or clubs, or dances, I suppose," I murmured vaguely.

They were horrified.

"But that is madness!" they cried "Marriage is a serious business. It requires much serious thought and discussion and investigation before a partner is chosen — someone with whom you have to share your whole life. . . ."

It began to occur to me that if I was to write realistically about these people I must not take it for granted that they would approach any subject with the same premise as me. As a result, I had to keep readjusting my thought processes, keep starting from scratch, so to speak. I had to practise thinking like someone who had been conditioned by totally different habits and standards and ideas from me.

I cannot stress enough what an invaluable discipline this is for a novelist. Writers like Tolstoy and Balzac perfected this ability to identify with others to an intense and total degree. Tolstoy successfully portrayed the whole panorama of Russian society. Balzac, "in competition with the Registrar of Births", entered on the record of mankind two thousand men and women of all types and walks of life.

It's that first premise that counts. It's the inward watchfulness that prevents you getting off on the wrong tack. It's that first leap across the bridge that enables you to see from an entirely different angle. It's the conscious effort needed to see the stranger with the same amount of patience, compassion and forgiveness as you would your own family or yourself. I agree with Arnold Bennett who said that the novelist's attitude towards his characters should be one of "Christ-like compassion".

However, despite the differences in language, customs and outlook, I found my new friends basically the same as me and any other folk I knew, and I believe that as long as we can cling to this idea of our common humanity or, as the Quakers say, "that of God (or good) in every man", then difficulties can and will be overcome. (As my mother used to say, "Where there's a will, there's a way.")

Unfortunately one of the things everyone seems to have in common, — and my Pakistani friends were no exception — is the tendency to nurse prejudices against sections of their fellow men and for the same reasons of lack of knowledge and understanding.

White people used to try to tell me that Pakistanis ate dog meat and did other things which didn't do much to encourage me to take them to my heart. But of course I discovered in fact that my friends who were Muslims were very particular about their meat. Like the Jews, they preferred their own butchers where the meat was bled in a special way and prayers were said over it. And they didn't eat pork because they considered it dirty.

They were most particular about personal cleanliness too. In fact, I'd never come across folk who washed so much!

But my Pakistani friends were prejudiced against Hindus and would say to me:

"Never have anything to do with Hindus, Margaret. They are

94

dirty people. They sprinkle cow's urine over everything in their houses. They worship the cow. They are also idolaters."

I'd never met any Hindus and I made a mental note that I didn't fancy them and would be very wary if I ever came across any. Then, one summer my husband and I went on a bus tour to Europe. We visited seven or eight different countries and ended up spending a week in the Austrian Tyrol. Now, right away, when our bus party set off I noticed this solitary Indian among us. He looked very shy and miserable hanging back in corner on his own. Think of how you'd feel yourself if it was the other way around, I told myself. How would you feel alone in India with nothing but coloured folk all around you and all talking away in a strange language? I find it's always a help to think along these lines and also to try to worry about people in the same way as you'd do with your own family. So I worried about this Indian feeling lonely and not understanding what the courier was saying and maybe forgetting his passport and not getting the kind of food his religion obliged him to eat and not being able to explain to anybody. Soon I overcame my own shyness and went over to him and asked him if he was getting the right food and if he was all right. I invited him to join our crowd of friends and generally took him under my wing. This, I learned, was his first trip out of India. He'd flown over for a short visit to his sister and brother-in-law in London and was now doing this coach tour to see Europe.

It turned out he was a Hindu. That shook me a little. Then I thought — well, we all have our funny little ways if you really got down to thinking about it. And what was a little cow's urine between friends? (Actually he was most fastidious. He was always disappearing away to his room to have a shower and change his clothes.)

We became good friends together, Sharad Babu and the rest of our little group. Many a good laugh we enjoyed together and what great talks we had. Sharad willingly answered all my questions about his customs and religion. I was most touched by his feelings about his wedding night. He said it was the most beautiful and treasured moment of his life when he first saw his wife's face. (It was an arranged marriage and he'd never seen her before the wedding.) But there happened to be two single beds in the room in which they spent the wedding night and he was too desperately shy at first to approach his wife's bed. He had a gift to give her as was the custom, a beautiful ring. But he took it to bed with him and just lay there on his own, fearfully anxious and wondering what to do.

Then, just as he was plucking up courage to leave his bed and go

95

across to his wife, he discovered he couldn't find the ring and had to rummage frantically about in the bed to try and recover it. Eventually he found his gift offering and the courage.

Later, when he got to know his wife better, he asked her how she had felt that night as they lay in separate beds and she replied:

"Very worried!" (Well, you can imagine!)

As I said, he answered all my questions about his religion too and soon I could see, from his point of view, Hinduism was just as reasonable a thing to believe in as the Muslim religion, or the Jewish, or the Catholic, or the Protestant. . . .

In fact, Sharad Babu just about converted us all, if not by his religion, at least by his charm and his enthusiastic and unsophisticated affection for us.

Although again, of course, there was the odd little language difficulty. Like when he told the young honeymoon couple of the party, Ruth and Ralph, that he fancied them. He just meant that he liked them very much. Then, of his room-mate Frank (who was a big Welshman) Sharad waxed wildly enthusiastic and said:

"Frank is so sweet and innocent. I love him!"

Actually there was an odd kind of naivety about big Frank and we knew what Sharad meant. Sharad in fact became so overcome with emotion about us all that he'd hug Frank and my husband and George — another member of our group of friends. Or he'd slap their knees or link arms with them and me while sitting on the long back seat of the coach as we careered along singing happily through all the different countries.

I'll never forget those spontaneous demonstrations of loving friendship between ordinary human beings who had somehow got over the dividing bridge of custom, religion and tradition and met on equal and trusting terms in the middle.

# CHAPTER EIGHTEEN

I HAD JUST finished the Pakistani novel when *The Breadmakers* trilogy was returned to me. Nine months the publisher had kept it before returning it.

So now I had five novels on my hands. (Actually I had *ten* novels because I'd already written another five, remember!) The only thing to do in a case like this is to immediately post one or other or all of them out again. That way you have always something to hope for. After all, you just might be lucky with the next publisher.

I decided to post away *The Prisoner* and the Pakastani novel first. I wanted to have another read at *The Breadmakers* trilogy to see if there was anything I could do to improve it. But where to send the two new novels? It sounds crazy but I decided to send them to the publisher who had just rejected my trilogy and for no other reason than his firm's name began with A and I thought I might as well work my way through the alphabet. Within a week I had a letter saying they had decided to publish my work and it was now only a matter of deciding which novel to do first and would I please send back the trilogy! After all these years — a lifetime — I get five novels accepted at once.

I was still living in Bearsden at the time and I had been along at the shops and was feeling none too sprightly as I slowly returned to the house trundling my shopping trolley behind me. I opened the front door and when I got into the hall I saw this letter lying on the floor. On picking it up I noticed it had a London postmark and I thought it would be an acknowledgement of delivery of my two books. When I opened it and saw what it said I actually leapt and danced around the hall like a dervish. Then I went dashing and shouting through the house but no one was in to share my good news. (This was the news, by the way, that was later met with complete silence by a gathering of relations.) I 'phoned several friends in mounting hysteria before I eventually found someone to whom I could babble out the miracle.

In double quick time I had the trilogy winging its way back to London and it was decided to bring out *The Breadmakers* first. Before it came into print, however, the publisher was on the telephone to me with a few queries. Up to that point I'd always taken it for granted that, although I was a Scotswoman, I spoke and wrote plain English. Not so! Before the publisher was finished asking what this word meant and that expression meant, I felt an absolute foreigner. I discovered that without even realizing it I had used many Scotticisms. I complied with the "translations" that the publisher suggested. All the same, I felt and still feel that the meaning was clear enough in the context of each passage. And, after all, I as a reader have to cope with books by English authors and Welsh authors and American authors.

But I have discovered that some London publishers and agents have a "thing" about Scotland and the Scots. I don't believe they really like us very much up here. They seem to have this idea we're a crowd of ignorant savages running about with razors hidden in our kilts! And they worry about the sale potential of a book set in Glasgow (the reason given by several publishers who turned the books down).

Well, I believe a good story is a good story no matter where it is set. And "a man's a man for a' that . . .".

It turned out that I was right. My books have all sold well. The Breadmakers trilogy has been reprinted. My books are selling in America and other countries abroad. There is still a waiting list for my books in all the libraries and in fact *A Baby Might Be Crying* was voted Top Book in one English library.

But before this, lots of other exciting things had happened. *The Breadmakers* was first published and I went to London and was wined and dined and interviewed by the press.

The paddle-steamer *Caledonia* had been featured in my book and it was discovered that this old ship was no longer plying up and down the Clyde but was sitting on the Thames in London. A party was arranged on board to which pressmen and magazine editors and paperback publishers came. It all seemed like a dream.

Even after I came home lots of journalists kept arriving on my doorstep to interview me. One interesting point that emerged from all these interviews (which were not about my book, by the way, but about me) was that on the whole, the articles seemed more a reflection of the journalist's character than mine. It seemed to me anyway that I was reading about a different person in each newspaper feature.

Some journalists had stronger personalities than others and I remember one lady, who was also taping our interview for radio, briefing me beforehand with:

"Now, I'll say — and then you'll say — And then I'll ask — and then you'll reply — and then I'll say — and then you'll say —"

Although I tried to remember and struggle to give all the answers she clearly thought I ought to give, my heart wasn't in it. The interview was a bit of a shambles and as far as I know was never accepted either for print or for radio.

My second book, *A Baby Might Be Crying*, had an even better reception and I was particularly glad about that, not only because it had been such hard work but also because that book meant a lot to me.

The third of the trilogy, *A Sort of Peace*, was hailed as the best of the three. By this time I was receiving letters from ordinary readers telling me they had enjoyed my books. Some also told me their life histories and all their problems. Some people even sent photographs of themselves. I came to the conclusion that there must be a great many lonely and troubled people about.

Hearing from readers and learning how much they appreciated my books made all the hard work worthwhile. Mark Twain said: "The public is the only critic whose opinion is worth anything at all." Maybe he's right, I don't know but it is certainly a great thrill and most heart-warming to hear from readers.

Next, the publisher suggested I write a historical novel set in Glasgow but if possible, with an American tie-up. At first I had a bit of a struggle with my integrity. I couldn't see how I could *believe* in what I was doing if I wrote this type of book.

I couldn't see how I could believe in characters, even imaginary characters who were supposed to live so long ago. They all seemed so dead and buried and pointless before I even started. And that's no way to feel when you write a book. Also I didn't think I was going to be at home with or in sympathy with Prince Charlie or wealthy tobacco or any other kind of lords. And if, as I suspected, the publisher wanted some kind of romantic view of history, that would go against my grain. Yet I'd promised to write a historical novel and write one I must.

I set off to the Mitchell Library and began reading about all the people and happenings of the time. Before long I found myself enthralled and the more I read, the more I gravitated towards the poorest folk of the time. With them I could identify. Soon my eighteenth-century characters were as vividly alive to me as anyone in *The Breadmakers* or in my contemporary novel *The Prisoner* had been. In the end, I not only enjoyed writing that book, I enjoyed the research almost as much. What fun I had reading some of the journals of ladies and gentlemen of the time. From them I picked up the rhythms of the speech and the favourite expressions and words they used. "Prodigious" kept cropping up for instance, so I made that a word my character, Annabella used a lot. "Fluttered" was another and it was most annoying when an editor changed it to "flustered". I firmly changed it back again. Annabella had definitely felt *fluttered*.

I laughted uproariously as I wrote certain scenes, just as I'd done while writing *The Breadmakers* trilogy. Other scenes made me sob brokenheartedly. I remember the first time I appeared with my face all tear-stained and swollen after writing a scene in *The Breadmakers*. My sons cried out in concern:

"What's wrong, Mum?"

I sobbed in reply: "Jimmy's just died."

"Who's Jimmy?" they wanted to know.

I had to explain that he was a character in my book. They groaned and rolled their eyes. It's a terrible trial having a writer as a mum.

In *The Prince and The Tobacco Lords* another character "took off" who I had only intended to be a very minor person in the book. Old Quin, the beggar, I don't know why, just grew and grew and there was no getting away from him. When he and I had to say goodbye there was a very painful lump in my throat. (Long after the book was finished I'd find myself wondering what happened to Quin.)

The second two books of that trilogy (again I found I couldn't fit the whole story into one book), *Roots of Bondage* and *Scorpion In The Fire*, are set half in Glasgow and half in America. Needless to say, the American research presented difficulties but I wrote to the Research Librarian in the University of Virginia who was most helpful. She also put me in touch with an American publisher who specialized in books about the period. As a result I obtained books like *Women's Life and Work in the Southern Colonies* and *Colonists in Bondage* and *The Secret Diary of William Byrd*. The latter was very amusing in places. William Byrd was in the habit of making entries in his diary like:

"I said a short prayer but notwithstanding I committed uncleanness in bed."

And: "I rogered my wife, I neglected to say my prayers but had boiled milk for breakfast."

And: "Gave my wife a flourish on the billiard table today."

The mind boggles!

American friends also helped me by sending research material.

For the Glasgow side, it was back to the old Mitchell Library again. I also had at one point to find out about a poison — belladonna or deadly nightshade. I had to know the effects it had if administered to someone. For this I had to go upstairs to a department of the library that I hadn't used before and in which I was not known. You should have seen the suspicious looks I got when I said I wanted to find out what exactly would happen if I gave someone a dose of deadly nightshade! Actually the symptoms of belladonna poisoning are particularly horrible and when I came to write the scene I really felt quite ill. I'm being perfectly serious about this. Writers suffer from emotional, physical and mental strains often with embarrassing and traumatic results.

# CHAPTER NINETEEN

YOUR SENSITIVITIES, your emotions, your mind, your nerves, everything has to be stretched to its limits while working. At the same time you've to be highly disciplined. For instance, you must organize regular *time* for writing. Time is vitally important. Warren Beaty said the best time to get married was at lunchtime — so that if it didn't work out you hadn't wasted the whole day!

I find the best time to write is in the morning. Although once a book really gets going I tend to write morning, afternoon and night with only dazed breaks in between to wash dishes, cook meals and go shopping. When I say dazed, I really mean dazed. How can I, after spending most of my waking hours back in eighteenth-century America for example, and in the guise of a dozen different characters, all with dramatic things happening to them, how can I *suddenly* become bright and sensible and alert in the twentieth century? I can't. Only the surface of my mind manages to function in the immediate world around me when I leave my desk and go along to the shops to buy some steaks and a bag of frozen potatoes. To me, the *real* world is the world of Annabella and Gav and Regina and Old Quin. I'm deeply involved and harrowed by what's happening to them. Who cares about steaks and frozen potatoes?

I remember one such occasion which became very embarrassing and upsetting. I was wandering along by the shops when I vaguely thought I heard someone calling my name. On gazing further down the road I saw at the front of a line of cars at the traffic lights, a man gesticulating frantically in my direction from the window of a green car. The scene registered no further than my eyes and even at that level it was misty because I'm short-sighted. Not until after I'd returned to the house and had a cup of tea did the urgency, the reality of the scene impress itself on my mind. Then I couldn't get back to my writing. I became too worried and anxious. Had an old friend been trying to contact me again? Had I hurt his feelings by ignoring him? It was no use, I just couldn't settle at my desk until I'd done something about my terrible behaviour. On an impulse I lifted the 'phone and dialled the small ads page of the Glasgow *Evening Times*. The advert I put in was nicely worded to the effect that I wanted to apologize to the man in the green car, and I gave my 'phone number.

At least six men 'phoned me to ask if they could come over and apologize to me! It might sound funny now but, believe me, at the time I was shaking like a leaf. They obviously thought I was a call-girl. One man said as much. It, temporarily at least, shattered my faith in men. I mean, it was a perfectly innocent advert, I still can't understand why these men reacted like that. I kept saying in shocked tremulous tones:

"I'm terribly sorry, I'm afraid you've made a mistake."

I suppose instead of being so polite I should just have said: "Piss off!" But I have this horror of conflict and nastiness and always long for people just to be nice to one another.

I suppose it's unrealistic of me. My son Calvin more or less accused me of that the other day. He was talking about a programme he had been watching on television. It was about the balance of nuclear power. The idea (the programme's, not Calvin's) was that we had to have the same amount of nuclear arms as the Russians to make them afraid to use their weapons. I was saying that I didn't feel any safer since we had Polaris missiles and God knows what on and around our shores. It was in fact, now being admitted that because of having all this here, we would now be *the prime target* in any war.

As a writer I find myself in a quandary about this subject.

The trouble is that I feel *so* passionately about these things, I get dangerously upset and depressed. I say — dangerously — because it is the only thing that nearly defeats my will to continue writing. It occurs to me, you see, that not only would people — men, women and innocent children — die horrible deaths in a nuclear war, but all art of all ages, including writing, would be wiped out forever. With this thought in mind it is hard to feel that it is worthwhile going on writing. But I can't help going on. It's just a case of — where there's life, there's hope I suppose.

I said to Calvin that if only Britain could get out of the arms race altogether and give the world a moral lead. If only we could think in more imaginative and human terms. If only we could get off the nightmare track of fear politics and learn to trust and to take more positive steps to try to understand each other's needs and backgrounds and motivations and to work constructively to help one another.

"Mum, you're talking about heaven!" Calvin cried out in exasperation.

"Well, I'm sick of the hell that politicians are creating," I said. "Anything's better than what they're leading us into."

The awful thing for me is that, as I've already indicated, when I read about or think about this subject, I feel and hear and see such horrifying *individual* suffering. I see the burned child in close-up. I hear it as if it was already screaming. I don't want to think about

103

it because of the distress and depression that nearly paralyses me. I want to be like an ostrich and hide my head from every hint in writing or talking or on television or film about the subject.

John Braine says in *Writing a Novel* (talking about being a writer):

> It is better, too, right from the first never to become associated with any political party or any cause, no matter how good. It is better, too, never to write letters to the papers, no matter how strongly one may feel. Let everything go into your writing; let your novel be the receptacle for all that you think and feel. I don't, of course, mean that your novel should express your political beliefs; for instance, that you have one of your characters write the letter to the paper on whatever is making you burn with emotion. I mean that if you don't speak at a public meeting, don't carry a banner in a demo, don't write a letter to the papers, the emotion itself will find its way into your novel.

I expect he's right. But still. . . .

I went on an anti-nuclear demonstration recently. The first I'd ever been on. I arrived early and was rather taken aback, first of all to see the large number of police on foot and on horseback, and secondly, to see the motley crowd of long-haired, lefty-looking youngsters waiting in the rain. Their banners boldly proclaimed things like, "Don't put us in a nuclear dustbin!" and, "In the event of a nuclear accident — kiss your children goodbye!" and: "If it's so bloody safe, why don't they bury it under London?"

At that point I seemed to be the only middle-aged, tidily-dressed person there. Then I noticed a grey-haired, respectable-looking couple hovering worriedly nearby. I heard them say apprehensively: "It's all young people!"

I know how they felt but I hope they eventually managed to take their courage in both hands and stick to what they believed was right. Surely it's not a case of politics (or appearances). It's a matter of survival.

As far as that march in Glasgow was concerned, lots of other people eventually turned up but even if it had been only young folk there and even if they'd all had long hair and tatty denims — so what? Thank God for the young people, I say.

I couldn't get that apprehensive, grey-haired couple out of my head I kept seeing the expression in their eyes, and their grey plastic raincoats, and the way they stood close together with arms linked.

I imagined them in their home getting ready to come to the

104

march. Had they been nervous, or hopeful, or excited? They looked a most respectable couple, not the kind of people who would want to push themselves into the public eye. Perhaps they had been desperately worried about the spread of nuclear power and hadn't known what to do about it until they'd seen the poster about the anti-nuclear demonstration. I hoped they eventually joined the march to encourage by their presence, other folk like themselves. I wondered if they'd have the stamina to last out the long miles. I kept thinking about them and worrying about them.

In fact, I know I'll never be free of these two perfectly ordinary individuals until I put them in a novel. *This merciless haunting is what writing is all about.*

Novelists need to and must look at individuals and take a curious and caring view. The main purpose of the novel is to explore the problems of the individual and a good writer is one who can set his uniqueness on our common experience. The paradox of all art is that it is particularly individual and yet universal.

In exploring problems the novelist will find some answers, or at least some sort of understanding, and as a result help people to understand one another. And this must include self-identification with, and trying to understand the traditions, historical background and feelings of Russian communists as well as Indian Hindus and Pakistani Muslims.

But talking to Calvin like that set me thinking about something else. All of a sudden I remembered that I used to get exasperated with my mother in exactly the same way.

She'd say things like: "If ordinary folk all over the world would lay down their arms and refuse to fight one another, there would be no more wars."

Or: "If all decent folk would just have the courage to say to their leaders — No, I will not raise a hand against my brother. . . ."

"If only . . . if only. . . . What's the use of that?" I used to say. "You're talking about hypothetical, idealistic situations!"

I had to admire her though because she had the courage of her convictions. During the war people used to come to all the doors asking for donations of anything metal to go towards the war effort. They would come to our door all smiling and unsuspecting and my mother would completely nonplus them by saying:

"No, I will not give you one nail to help make a bullet to kill any mother's son!"

Sometimes the collectors would indignantly retaliate but my mother soon made short work of them.

My point is, however, that when my mother used to argue with me, I used to feel the very same about her as my sons now feel about me.

That shakes me!

You know how you always feel young inside? (At least I do.) I mean, you're still the child you always were, you're still everything you always were. The only person you don't feel inside is an old person. It's only your body that gets old.

But that conversation with Calvin gave me a jolt. This means I'm getting old, I thought. First it was my mother's turn and now it's mine. It's the natural progression of things. Fancy me getting *old*! At one time this would have profoundly depressed me. In this nuclear age, however, getting old isn't depressing any more. I have and you have, a *right* to get old, to live out our span on earth. It's only too short as it is.

I pray that I'll be allowed to grow old. I pray that Calvin too will follow the natural progression of things and one day his son or daughter will get exasperated with him, and one day he will grow old.

I pray that my son Kenneth, who is at the beginning of his marriage to a lovely girl called Arlene, will be allowed to go through all the natural stages of life too. Last year Ken and Arlene moved into a nice, two-bedroomed semi-detached house in a country area outside of Glasgow. He has a garden for the first time in his life and he was on the 'phone only yesterday in great excitement because the flowers he'd planted were beginning to show buds. And he's going to get a raise in his wages.

"Arlene says, Mum, that this means maybe in a year we'll be able to start a family!"

The tremble of joy in his voice, his eagerness in looking forward to a happy future made me close my eyes and pray in secret to all the governments in the world:

"Oh, please, let my son have his future."

What goes wrong with men and women when they get into governments — all governments, including our own? Does power blunt their humanity, their understanding, their imaginations, not to mention their common sense?

It looks to me as if power does indeed corrupt, and it is left now to you and to me, to the elderly people in the grey plastic raincoats, and to the young people, to somehow get back to basics. We'll have to cling to our unique yet common humanity and each of us do what we can.

People need their time to live and writers need their time to write.

Novelists need *regular* time. The creative part of the brain becomes more efficient with regular exercise. To keep to regular working hours it helps to act as if you have a boss keeping an eagle eye on when you start. After all, you wouldn't turn up an hour or more late at any other place of business and expect to get away with excuses like: "I was too tired to think about work today." Or: "After I made the beds and washed the dishes etc. there wasn't much time for anything else." Or: "I just wasn't in the mood." You would soon be told that that wasn't good enough and sent packing. It's not good enough for a writer either.

Once you take yourself firmly in hand and decide what hours you are going to work, the next problem is to ensure that your family and friends allow you peace to get on with it. You've got to discipline other people as well as yourself.

I managed fairly quickly to get my friends into the habit of 'phoning me in the afternoons or evenings instead of the mornings. I did this by stating quite categorically that because I worked from 9–1 they would have to avoid calling during these hours. If this didn't work at first and someone did telephone to indulge in ordinary social chit-chat, I was polite and patient but rather quiet. I was only my usually chatty self during afternoon or evening calls. Or, I'd interrupt my morning caller in as kindly a tone as possible to say:

"Look, I wonder if you'd mind calling back this afternoon? I'd be free to enjoy a talk with you then."

Or words to that effect.

If it was someone in some sort of distress or seriously in need of a friend to talk to then of course that was different. But most times it was just for a wee blether.

My mother was the most frequent offender.

When I was writing *The Prince and the Tobacco Lords* I would be sitting in my writing-room willing myself backwards in time until at last my mind would start flickering with candlelight. I would hear the clatter of horses' hooves outside. I was Annabella Ramsay in my house in the Trongate. The Trongate is busy with people going to the dancing assembly. I'm ready in my hooped skirt, high wig, and face patches. I'm impatiently agitating my fan and wishing that my maid Nancy would come and tell me that my sedan chair is ready.

Pap frowns on such frivolities as dancing assemblies.

"Annabella," he said. "I forbid you to go to that den of iniquity!"

I flung myself about. I kicked and screamed and created such a fuss until he agreed, in case I took a fit or worse. Papa spoils me. He acts fierce. He threatens to order the doctor to give me a good bleeding or the hangman to whip me through the streets. And one day. . . .

107

A bell rings. My hand gropes out for it. Someone says in my ear:

"Is that you, Margaret? I just thought I'd tell you that Sadie dropped in to see me last night. The reason she didn't manage on Monday was because her car broke down."

Eh? Margaret? Sadie? Who are they? A car? What's this? My mind fumbles and gropes back through the mists of time. Horses' hooves fade away and disappear. So does my beautiful gown, my wig with the strings of lammer beads looped over it. So does my elegant fan, and my jewelled snuff-box. There is no longer any sensation of anything.

The mist clears. I see bookshelves, a filing cabinet, a desk, white paper, a pen in one hand, a telephone in the other. I remember who Sadie is.

"Oh, yes, how is Sadie, Mum? I've never seen her for ages. Oh? Oh. Piles. Oh, dear. Yes. Painful things. Uh — huh. Oh, the poor soul! Oh, fancy! Isn't that terrible? Oh, I know. See doctors! Uh — huh. Oh, isn't that awful. . . ."

My mind is now full of Sadie's sufferings and it takes quite a struggle to banish her, and her piles from my thoughts. I'm also left with the irritation of my mother's now constant and anxious query of: "Are you all right?"

Talk of Sadie was only an excuse. Since the death of my brother and my father, my mother had developed an anxiety complex and a terror of being alone.

# CHAPTER TWENTY

MAYBE THE truth was my mother had never liked to be on her own. Certainly she had always been a very gregarious person. Sometimes, looking back, I think she missed her vocation and should have been an actress. Immediately a visitor arrived or immediately she joined a gathering of people it was as if she stepped into a spotlight. Her face lit up. Her brown eyes sparkled. She held herself like a queen. She spoke confidently and entertainingly. She told funny anecdotes. She played the piano. She sang songs. If there was a violin or any other instrument in the place she had a go at that too. It wasn't that she was a show-off or in any way boastful. In fact it wasn't until after my mother died that I discovered that she was actually qualified to teach music and was an LRAM.

I never knew her to have any patience for reading music far less to carry it around. If anyone asked if she could play a particular piece she'd just say:

"Certainly! How does it go?"

The enquirer would find themselves having to try to hum or whistle anything from "Mares-eat-oats-and-does-eat-oats" to Beethoven's Fifth. After a few bars my mother would brush them impatiently aside with, "Och, aye!" before plunging from one end of the keyboard to the other in an energetic and impressive flourish. No key was left unused. Then she would give a spirited rendering of whatever piece had been requested.

She enjoyed bursting forth into song as well, some of her favourites being "Bless This House", "The Old Rugged Cross", "If I Can Help Somebody" and "Abide With Me".

It never worried her if she forgot the words halfway through. Without as much as a pause for breath she made up words of her own to fit in, and just as smoothly transferred to the right words once they came back to her. It was the same with music. If she went wrong in a piece or forgot the tune, she stamped her foot defiantly down on the loud pedal and flung her fingers about in a crescendo of chords or merry ripples until she remembered the original melody. I used to sit in an agony of suspense waiting for bits of Chrissie Thomson to suddenly break into Robert Burns or Chopin. It was bad enough in the private houses of friends. In front of an audience in a church hall, or YMCA meeting, or charity concert, or at any public gathering, it was absolute torture. Only to me, I hasten to make clear! Everyone else seemed to thoroughly enjoy the performance. My mother was always perfectly convinced they did anyway.

It was just as nerve-racking when she spoke in public. She would never prepare her talk, never give it a thought, never take a note. She would just sail up to the platform and start to speak without turning a hair.

In answer to my queries about what she was going to talk about she'd say: "Och, I expect I'll tell them one of my wee stories!"

She meant anecdotes from her own life. Or sometimes she'd tell the audience in her own words about a book or story she'd read and enjoyed. The anecdotes were either funny or romantic or both. The stories were invariably sentimental. It always seemed to me incredible — not only that she could rise to any occasion so effortlessly (if a speaker didn't turn up and she happened to be in the audience she never had any hesitation in rising if asked — or even if not asked — and offering to save the day) but that she could talk in such a rosy, romantic vein. The chances were, not half an hour before, she would have been bitterly battling with my father.

For my part, I would be feeling sick and shaken and harrowed. I would be completely worn out with just having listened to the quarrelling. Sometimes I used to become seriously confused as well. It was as if I was not only losing a grip of life around me, but of myself. I used to wonder what was real and who was real. Could the world of conflict inside our house just be a figment of my imagination? Was my mother actually the happy, romantic person I saw when she was in the company of other people?

This kind of experience stood me in good stead when I eventually became a novelist. I never take anyone at their face value now. Nothing really surprises me as far as human relationships are concerned. I have a wide-open mind, ready and waiting, and curious, to see what's going on behind the mask, or behind the net curtains. People all put forward a certain image of themselves in normal social contacts. So often this gives a very mistaken picture of what they or their lives are really like. It's a novelist's job to recognize the difference between what people say — the image they project of themselves — and what they *do* and *are*.

My mother still had a wonderful spirit — in company at least — after my brother died. But her black hair began to go white and thin and her shoulders became more rounded. She hadn't the same, if any, interest in her appearance. She used to like a nice hat and had always been extremely proud of an apple-green straw boater she'd picked up at a jumble sale for sixpence. I remember a red felt one she was rather fond of which blew off one day and went

110

right under the wheels of a bus. After the bus went over it, she picked it up, punched it back into shape and put it on again.

She had always argued with my father (I've heard him cry out: "I can't say black without you saying white!") but now, it seemed to me, a bitterness she could no longer control, an absolute hatred of my father engulfed her, seethed continuously under the surface of her relationship with him. I may be wrong. I hope I'm wrong. After all, how can I, or anyone really, truly know another person, know their emotions, know what *makes* them feel as they do, know the secret struggle they might be having with themselves?

But I sometimes suspected my mother hated my father even to touch her or go near her after my brother died. Yet, she wouldn't allow him to sleep in a separate room, although he kept being wakened during the night either by my mother getting up to go to the bathroom or to make herself a cup of tea because she couldn't sleep. Then when she did sleep she kept him awake with her snoring. He had his work to go to next day and he was getting quite frantic with fatigue. But she wouldn't let him go. (Not that there was anywhere to go except the living-room sofa. They didn't have another bedroom or front room in this house. They didn't even have a bed-settee.)

It seemed even then she couldn't bear to be alone.

From the day my father died, two of my cousins who were nurses stayed with her night and day because she refused to spend a moment alone in the house. She would have given the house up the day after the funeral if I hadn't persuaded her to wait for a few months before making any decisions about what she was going to do or where she was going to live. I told her she would be welcome to stay with me until she got over the shock of my father's death and could think about things more calmly and clearly.

That first day when she arrived at my house in Bearsden and I took her up to the bedroom I'd made ready for her, she looked around and said wistfully: "I could stay here for the rest of my life."

My brain keeps blanking out now. I try to turn my mind's eye inward to examine myself and the events that followed but it's as if there's a wall blotting out memories. I strain against it until my head aches yet nothing comes to me through the blackness except a very few disjointed scenes.

I remember when she first saw the room. I remember the slight relaxing of her muscles. She looked as if she thought she was safe. The room was very small, no more than a narrow box-room. The bigger room at the back which had been my father-in-law's bed-sitting-room was much larger. Since he had died however, it had been converted into a writing-room for me. It now contained office furniture and bookshelves packed with reference books. But I had tried to make the small room as pleasant as possible, with a pretty bedmat and rug and pictures on the wall and a vase of flowers on the chest of drawers. It was bright, that was what mattered to my mother. She could never at any time stand dark dull places and she could never bear the colour black. Even at the funerals of my brother and my father she could not bring herself to wear anything black. The room also faced the front and was cheery with the noise of traffic and people. But, most important of all, through the wall in the next room was where I slept.

She must have been in a very bad state of nerves by this time although she never complained and still in company she was, to all appearances, her normal cheery self. I remember, though, the first morning I went to give her a cup of tea in bed, I couldn't get the bedroom door opened. I couldn't understand it and after calling to her, I heard loud thumping and scraping noises. When my mother eventually opened the door I discovered that she'd had the chest of drawers jammed up against it to secure it shut. Every night I'd hear her lock herself in and pull the furniture up against the door.

I can only bring to mind two other scenes from the six months during which my mother lived with me. And even those are not too clear. One was when Kenneth was either being mildly disobedient or cheeky to me (it couldn't have been anything serious because Calvin and Kenneth have always been good boys) and my mother started talking to him as she used to talk to me about how God worked in strange and terrible ways.

"One day He'll take your mammy away from you," she told Kenneth. "You'll never see her again. Then you'll wish you hadn't spoken to her like that."

I immediately exploded in her astonished face. I was shivering violently with emotion.

"Don't you dare speak to him like that! Never speak to him like that again, do you hear?"

Hurt and bewilderment replaced her surprise. Tears shimmered in her eyes.

"But I was only sticking up for you," she said.

I was beyond myself, stuttering with the violence of my emotions, incapable of channelling them into lucid expression.

"You're not going to make him suffer with guilt. You're not going to do to him what you did to me. I won't let you!"

Afterwards I felt more wretched with guilt than I'd ever done in my life. The poor soul had lost her son and her husband. The last thing she needed was me shouting at her as if I hated her. I tried to be extra loving to make up for it and she immediately gratefully forgave me.

I began to have some inkling of the terrible conflict of emotions she had suffered while living with my father towards the end of his life. I began to be torn with conflicting emotions myself. I struggled frantically to keep them secret from her. The worse I felt inside, the calmer and more loving I forced myself to act.

And I did love her. I always will love her.

I weep now as I write. I don't know why.

I can only remember one other scene. It was New Year's Eve. We call it Hogmanay in Scotland and it's the custom to "stay up for the bells" and to either go out "first-footing" or welcome any visitors who arrive to "first-foot" you after midnight. Whisky and wine and cake and shortbread are made ready and the family all wait for the chimes of midnight. Then they all kiss each other and wish each other a Happy New Year.

It's unheard of to go to bed before midnight and not be with your family to bring in the New Year. But I couldn't face it. I just couldn't. Perhaps I was worn out beyond endurance with nursing my father-in-law. I often think that if I hadn't had him — and, after all, he'd been with me all my married life — I would have had enough emotional and physical energy to cope with my mother and look after her for the rest of her life. By this time, you see, she had given up her house. The day she walked out of it to come to me she had said:

"I'll never live here again." And she was true to her word.

Maybe it was the strain of having to cope with my mother's inability to be left on her own, even for a few minutes in a room, that was too much for me. She followed me about the house during the day. I could no longer go into my writing-room. It was even a worry to get to the toilet. If I went shopping she had to hurry and get ready and go out too. At night it was impossible to leave her in the house. She had to either have a friend come and see her or she had to go and visit a friend. And she was getting less and less able to go out.

That New Year, the first since my father's death, I just went up to bed the back of eleven, shut my eyes and pulled the bedclothes over my head.

I heard the bells. I heard the clink of glasses. I heard my mother and my husband wishing each other a Happy New Year. Knowing what he thought of my mother I marvelled at him being able to carry on the charade.

That's all I can remember. But my mother must have known that the situation couldn't continue because it was after that she started talking about going into an old folks' home.

113

# CHAPTER TWENTY-ONE

IN *THE PRISONER*, the springboard I'd used for the character of Celia had been a friend who was rather a weak as well as an unhappy woman. Celia was secretly relying more and more on drugs and drink, at the same time as desperately trying to keep up her respectable, conventional middle-class image to the outside world.

I'm not a drinker myself and only have the odd one or two in company to be sociable. But I avoid even that if I can because alcohol tends to upset my stomach. I was reminded once again though, after that book came out, of how people don't understand the way that characters in fiction are created. At a weekend conference I was attending in a hotel, a man discovering who I was, cornered me to tell me how much he had enjoyed *The Prisoner*. I was pleased and grateful for his appreciation but got slightly harassed when he insisted in shepherding me into the bar and buying me a drink. It was early in the forenoon and I'd far rather have had a cup of a tea.

"Whisky? Gin?" he kept pressing me.

Eventually I agreed to an orange juice. He looked taken aback, cheated even.

"But I got the distinct impression you liked your tipple," he said.

Admittedly there was something of me in Celia, as there was something of me, or people I knew, or had heard of, in every character in that book and in all my books. But, as in all my books, the truest thing is the emotion. And I felt Joe's emotion and Al's emotion and Wendy's emotion every bit as much as Celia's.

Maugham says:

> A group of characters, generally suggested by persons they (the novelists) have known, excites their imagination and sometimes simultaneously, sometimes after an interval, an incident, or a string of incidents, experienced, heard or invented, appears to them out of the blue to enable them to make suitable use of it in the development of the theme that has arisen in their minds by a sort of collaboration between the characters and the incidents.

Emotion is the keynote for creative writers. Whether it is excitement, or love, or hate, or greed, or compassion — it doesn't matter. The basic criterion to judge art is the honesty of its

114

emotion and in its relation to real life. D.H. Lawrence said that the important thing about novels is that they convey a sense of life — not abstract statements or concepts about life but an actual "tremulation" which conveys to the reader a sense of what life is. Novels evoke this sense of life by conveying or revealing relationships. The value of the novel as of all art lies in the fact that it is "life-conveying". But you must keep in mind that the artist makes something new and original through his own individuality; his own way of looking at people and events, his own way of feeling towards them.

He is also a teller of tales. His ancestor was the caveman sitting with his fellows round the open fire. He was the one who captured their attention and diverted it from the hardships and dangers of the world outside the cave — often by exaggerating these things and making them sound more fascinating, more orderly, or by making them happen to somebody else. But first he had to capture the attention of these restless people round the fire.

Sometimes it's a good test to think of yourself as that kind of storyteller among a crowd of disinterested people. You're going to open your mouth and say something and it's got to immediately rivet their attention, then hold their interest until you finish. It doesn't matter what kind of tale you're telling or if you're telling it to one person or to a multitude, the important thing is — it must not be boring.

The trouble with a novel is that events often need to be separated by a lapse of time and for the balance of the work, matter has to be inserted to fill up the lapse. These passages are known as bridges and they must be handled skilfully if they are to avoid being tedious. One way is to write charming narrative to show the passage of time. Describe a setting, a room, a house, a street, the countryside through the eyes of one of your characters. The description must also enhance or elucidate, or characterize, or bring a scene or person to life, to be relevant and helpful in some way to the story.

Another way is to make a leap in time when you start a new chapter but always remember to make it clear to the reader when and where you are in the new chapter if you make a jump in time.

One thing you should try to avoid describing *directly* is emotion. For instance, anger is an abstract term. You don't sit and think — I'm angry. You think things like — That swine, fancy doing that to me!

C.S. Lewis advises:

> Instead of telling us the thing was "terrible" describe it so that we'll be terrified. Don't say it was "delightful" make us

115

say, "Delightful" when we're reading the description. You see, all these words (horrifying, wonderful, hideous, exquisite) are only saying to your readers — "Please, will you do my job for me?"

Don't *say* a character is good or bad but instead select an incident in which he *shows* himself to be bad or good. Cast him in a dramatic scene. In other words rather than describe your characters — challenge them!

With practice these things eventually become instinctive. I don't say you stop making mistakes. It's a continuous struggle to keep trying to do what you believe is the right thing in writing, as in life. But it isn't until you are freed from the necessity of giving the greatest part of your attention to the mechanics of an art that you can really use that art as a channel for your creative power.

If you want to write a novel you should learn about the mechanics. You should read books by writers about the craft of fiction-writing. You should read books about the lives of writers. It all helps. But if you really want to write, you should WRITE. It will all click into place, it will come eventually with practice.

Some publishers say you should be able to give them a plot sentence or paragraph which tells them what your book is about (or is going to be about). One agent is on record as saying he "sells the sizzle not the steak". In other words a good plot sentence or paragraph or a briefly stated idea is what he insists he must have.

This is worth keeping in mind. It's good discipline too. And it helps if you remember that books are about people — people with problems. So first of all you should get sorted out in your mind whose story it has to be and what their problem is.

Art is a balance between discipline and freedom and I believe that when you write the first draft of your book you must be as free as a bird and totally uninhibited.

Peter Wastberg, talking about threats to a writer's freedom, made a very important point:

> Finally, the threat against a writer's freedom comes from within: he likes to please to gain readers, not to insult. He may be too embarrassed to express himself without inhibitions because of his family or his social commitments. An inhibited writer goes nowhere unless his very inhibitions are his subject matter. To write is to indulge in an intentionally promiscuous communication.

As I've said before, as you're writing, you keep thinking of better, clearer ways to convey what's in your mind. I always read

116

the previous day's work every morning to remind me of where I am and what's going on. As I do so I usually notice a few superfluous adjectives that need scoring out, or a verb that could be stronger, or a part where my pen's run away with me and I've repeated myself. I dash my pen through these bits. (Actually I use a pencil with a rubber on the end now so I normally rub things out rather than score them out.) But when writing that first draft I don't worry unduly about these things and certainly a beginner should not.

I say this because of a point I made in an early chapter. So many people who want to write (and remember, that's the first necessity: you must *want* to write) are fearfully inhibited by one thing or another and, as a result, they end up by simply not being able to do it at all. I knew one woman who could never get past a first paragraph. Honestly, she kept changing it and polishing it and rewriting it and could never get it as she thought it should be and after a few weeks she'd get so sick of these first few sentences she'd abandon the whole project. This used to infuriate me because it seemed such a waste. She got such good ideas, you see. A few months later she'd get another exciting idea for another story and she'd start doing the same thing again until eventually she whittled her self-confidence and her creativity away to nothing. Now she just makes excuses about not having the time and never writes at all.

I tell people like that (especially my over-sensitive, over-critical academic friends):

Say to yourself that *no one need ever see what you're writing.* It's completely private to you so *you have no need to worry.* You can let yourself go. To use vulgar parlance — you can let it all hang out! It doesn't matter if it seems a whole lot of rubbish. It doesn't even matter if it's ungrammatical. Nothing matters at all except that you should *get something written;* that you should get an uninhibited flow.

Once you've reached fifty thousand words or sixty, seventy or a hundred thousand or whatever length you like and have put the words THE END, then you've done it! You've written a book, it might be a lousy book but so what? *You've done it!* You've written a book. Plenty of time now to put it aside for a while. Rest on your laurels. Have a good think. Then, when you go back to your desk, you've got a book to work on, to rewrite if necessary. Or to tighten up or polish up.

Perhaps at this stage, or after a second draft, you might find it helpful to get the reaction of a couple of friends. But only if you have enough money to carry on writing no matter what they say.

You must not allow yourself to be crushed or discouraged by anyone. You must keep working on that book. Or, if you prefer, start work on another one. A writer is a person who writes and keeps on writing.

By the way, what do you think makes a good novel? Maugham claimed that the qualities of a good novel are as follows:

> It should have a widely interesting theme, by which I mean a theme interesting not only to a clique, whether of critics, professors, highbrows, bus-conductors or bar-tenders, but so broadly human that its appeal is to men and women in general; and the theme should be of enduring interest: the novelist is rash who elects to write on subjects whose interest is merely topical. When they cease to be so, his novel will be as unreadable as last week's newpaper. The story the author has to tell should be coherent and persuasive; it should be the natural consequence of the beginning. The episodes should have probability and should not only develop the theme, but grow out of the story. The creatures of the novelist's invention should be observed with individuality, and their actions should proceed from their characters. . . . And just as behaviour should proceed from character, so should speech. . . . It should serve to characterize the speakers and advance the story.
>
> The narrative passages should be vivid, to the point and no longer than is necessary to make the motives of the persons concerned, and the situations in which they are placed, clear and convincing. The writing should be simple enough for anyone of fair education to read with ease. . . . Finally, a novel should be entertaining . . . it is the essential quality, without which no other quality avails. And the more intelligent the entertainment a novel offers, the better it is.

(And, remember, entertainment means many things including *interest*.)

Of course, there are times when every author gets a mental blockage and doesn't seem to be able to write anything at all. My advice is don't panic. It's only a temporary phenomenon and, as I say, it happens to all of us.

First, make sure that you're not overtired or undernourished. I really mean this. You've got to be fit for writing. I see that I get a decent sleep. If necessary I take a hot drink sweetened with honey and four calcium tablets plus a herbal tranquillizer like "Quiet Life". I find honey great at any time during night or day. "Quiet Life" and "Passiflora" tablets are most helpful during the day too if you're feeling nervy or overstrained and of course you need

118

plenty of vitamin B for that.

I also take a regular daily multi-vitamin capsule or tablet (purchased from my local health food shop) and also Vitamin E and a B complex and a vitamin C. But the best general tonic and energy booster I have found is a course of Royal Jelly from the Organic Food Service in South Devon. Vitamin tablets etc. are of course only a *supplement* to a well-balanced diet. This means you should try your best, without being fanatical or faddy about it, to eat a little fresh or dried fruit, some raw vegetables (a mixed salad) and cooked vegetables and some protein (fish, meat, eggs, etc.) every day. The main thing is to try to keep to natural wholesome food and avoid white flour and white sugar. Use wholewheat flour and natural brown sugars and honey instead.

I wish I'd known all this years ago. It has made all the difference to my health.

Yoga is very good too — done gradually and gently.

If I've had a late night and haven't had enough sleep, I know there isn't much use pushing myself. (Although I admit I often do.) It's best to give up trying to do any fresh creative writing. Instead, I perhaps read back over what I have previously written and do a bit of correcting and cutting (although this has its dangers because if you're terribly drained and exhausted you might take a distorted, jaundiced view of your work). Or I retype a bit that needs neater presentation. Or I tidy my desk or my filing cabinet. Or I do any job *in my writing-room* that needs to be done even if it is something like hoovering the carpet.

Then I go and lie down in bed and try to completely relax for an hour or two, or if possible, sleep. And I vow that I will not have another late night until after my novel is safely finished.

However, if you have not been burning the candle at both ends and if you have made sure, as far as you can, that you are fit, and you still have a mental blockage, there's still no need to panic. It may be that you need a little treat, or a change of scene, or some stimulating company to excite you and recharge your batteries. I have tried this — even if it only meant a walk round town gazing at people and doing the same while I enjoyed a cup of tea and a normally forbidden cream cake in a restaurant — but I have tried it during the afternoon rather than take time off from my stricter forenoon hours of work. The danger with that course of action is, you see, that you might start making it an excuse to dodge off shutting yourself alone in your room to write.

What I usually do is to stick to my desk and write something, anything to start the flow of words again.

Emerson said he wrote a letter to a friend that he loved. I've

119

tried letters too. But mostly I just plod on with a bit of description to get me going. It's amazing how this stirs things up again.

Steinbeck says:

> Abandon the idea that you're ever going to finish. Don't think of 400 pages, only of writing one page for that day. Write anything as rapidly and freely as possible. Never correct or rewrite until the whole thing is down. Rewrite in process is usually an excuse for not going on. It also interferes with flow and rhythm which can only come from a kind of unconscious association with the material. Don't think of a generalized audience. Pick out one person and write to that one. If one scene or section gets the better of you — bypass it and go on.

Alexander Cordell says: "If you're stuck for something else to happen, bring in another character."

Every writer finds his own way through the wood. And you must find your way. All I'm saying is: there is a way — so don't lose heart, don't lose self-confidence and don't, whatever you do, give up.

# CHAPTER TWENTY-TWO

I HAVE A TAPE of my father telling my sons a story when they were small. But I haven't played it since he died. I don't think I could bear it. Not yet.

I remember the occasion. It was in our house in Cardonald and the boys had a tiny cam-ceiled room upstairs. The idea of the tape-recording was that on the evenings when "Pappa" wasn't there, the boys would still be able to hear him tell one of his stories. I insisted however (or was it my mother?) that he shouldn't get them all over-excited or they'd never be able to sleep so it had not to be one of his hair-raising tales. A storybook called *Timothy Tiptoes* was handed to him with the firm instruction:

"Now, Daddy, none of your carry-on. Read this quietly to them and no nonsense!"

Then I switched on the tape-recorder and left the bedroom. Before I'd reached the foot of the stairs I heard the children's giggles swirling into hysterical hilarity. I could imagine the funny faces my father would be pulling and the mock seriousness of his rendering of *Timothy Tiptoes*.

Whatever he was doing it was causing a riot and I marched back upstairs to give him a stern ticking off. On my return journey to the bedroom I could hear his conspiratorial giggles and whispers competing with those of the children. He was a "natural" with youngsters. He seemed to become one of them and was accepted as such. Yet at the same time he was adored as one big, crazy, fun person. And not only with his grandchildren. Always, but especially in the last house in which he lived, there was a constant stream of small children — some mere toddlers — knocking on the door and asking my mother if Sam was in. Or, because he sometimes took them to the park, they'd ask if Sam was coming out to play. They never called him Mr Thomson or even Uncle Sam — just Sam. Yet he could be such a shy, awkward, often quite embarrassing man with adults.

I have also a tape-recording of my mother's voice. She is singing her favourite songs and accompanying herself on the piano. I don't have the courage to listen to that either. I recorded it while she was in the old folks' home.

She didn't want to go there. Oh, she pretended she did. She fooled us into thinking she did. I think she even fooled herself. She was always such an optimist, you see. And she not only told rose-coloured, happy-ever-after stories, she *believed* them. She seemed as if she was looking forward to the big day, as if she was going on her holidays. She chatted to everyone about the place as if it was a first-class hotel on the Riviera. And everybody was so nice there, she kept repeating. My mother always spoke of everyone as if they wore haloes and had wings under their coats.

The home was a big, old villa in the west end of the city. The furniture in the sitting-room was big and old too, but beautifully polished. Everything was spotlessly clean and tidy. The bedrooms were in a modern extension at the back and they were tiny but each inmate had one to themselves. The sick-bay was also in the extension.

My mother kept stressing, and I kept agreeing, that she would be perfectly free to come and go as she liked. I said I would visit her regularly every week and she could come and visit me as often as she liked. After all, it was only about a twenty-minute bus run away. It seemed a very happy arrangement. It wasn't until the day came for her to leave our house in Bearsden that the truth dawned on me. She was frightened. Never before in my life had I seen my mother look frightened. Even as my brother lay dying she had shown no fear, only tragic resignation. Each time she left my brother's bedside she told me she just said to God: "Thy will be done."

But now her eyes were alert with apprehension and despite the proud tilt to her head, a pulse kept fluttering in her neck. My husband and I took her in the taxi. She was unusually silent.

The elderly matron greeted us kindly and showed us to the bedroom allocated to my mother. We deposited my mother's suitcase on the chair beside the bed and then followed matron to the sitting-room to be introduced to all the other old ladies and gentlemen.

Introductions over, I kissed my mother and told her she would be all right and not to worry, I'd see her next day. I waved her goodbye from the room doorway and said that once I got outside I'd wave up to the window. But once I got downstairs and outside I heard the piano belting out a "Scottish Selection". She had already forgotten all about me and was hell-bent on livening up the melancholy-looking, lethargic lines of elderly inmates. This new purpose in life kept her going at first and she regained much of her confident and cheerful manner. None of these people had heard any of her stories, nor her repertoire of songs and tunes and she was able to work her way through the whole gamut. Soon she had gathered new stories, and the picture she used to paint of the house was invariably kind but often hilarious — The little romances that

122

sprung up and how the ladies competed for the interest of a new gentleman resident. The fascinating lives some of the ladies had led in their youth. The sparkling wit of some of the gentlemen.

It always came as a shock to me when I visited my mother and she took me upstairs to the sitting-room and I saw the lines of chairs facing the television, the rows of white heads and bent backs; the sadness of it all.

But the matron and my mother were great friends and my mother seemed to find comfort and security in this relationship.

It must have been a sad blow to my mother when that matron retired and left the city.

She remained to all outward appearances as cheerful as ever, but her health deteriorated. She had "internal troubles" which became progressively more painful and debilitating. Her strong, independent spirit began to clash with the new people in authority. She refused, for instance, to take the tranquillizers and sleeping pills that were dished out and that, as far as I could see, kept everyone half-asleep during the day and unconscious during the night.

I used to urge her to take them, pointing out that she was getting strained and anxious with lack of sleep. This, in turn was causing headaches and all sorts of other distressing symptoms. The tranquillizers would make life easier for her (*for her?*) and soothe away her anxieties. But no, she wouldn't take them. It was a matter of defending her rights and her dignity as a free human being. Her spirit simply rebelled against joining those lines of zombies.

It made her an awkward ripple however, in the smooth-running sleepy pond of a place.

When she became acutely ill she insisted on going to the hospital of *her* choice. She had been a believer in homeopathy for a lifetime and it was to the Glasgow Homeopathic Hospital that she wished to go.

It's only recently that alternative treatment of this type has become more acceptable. Even yet, I suspect, the more traditional bastions of medicine (or at least some representatives of them) still harbour a sneering and belittling attitude towards it.

I can remember when my mother returned from the hospital. She had to convalesce for a few days in the home's sick bay and I had come back with her in the ambulance and waited while she was comfortably tucked into bed by the matron. Then, over my mother's bed the matron read aloud the instructions the hospital had sent regarding treatment; and she tittered. I saw my mother's quick, hurt look and frail though she was, she managed to speak up in defence of homeopathic treatment and of the Homeopathic

123

Hospital. The matron adopted a subtle, patronizing attitude, agreeing with her and treating her kindly as if she was an idiot child.

My mother made a few more pointed remarks backed up with facts and figures that showed she was anything but an idiot and what's more, was not going to be treated like one.

She recovered enough strength to get up and about again and although she was now wrinkled and bent and her hair was thin as well as white, she could still step into the spotlight and put on a splendid act like the tough old trouper that she was. I would look out my window in Bearsden and there she would be struggling along the road to come and visit me. We never missed a day of seeing each other. (She 'phoned me every day as well. Often more than once.) If I couldn't get in to see her, she came to see me. If my husband was in, he would drive her back to the home in his taxi. Sometimes, on the way, he would buy her a box of sweeties. She had a terrible sweet tooth. Any kindness from anyone she appreciated wholeheartedly but especially any kindness from us.

I still have a letter here in my mother's dashing hand. (Her handwriting never became spidery or weak despite her age or physical weakness.) The letter, written after one occasion when my husband had given her a lift, says:

> I just had to write this letter to try to express my appreciation for your great kindness.
>
> I hope and pray that when your evening comes and Margaret's that you will both have the love and care that I have received from yourselves and I have faith you will. God hears and knows even our unspoken prayers.
>
> Thanking you once again,<br>love,<br>Mum.

I eventually moved from Bearsden to a flat only ten minutes' walk away from the home. I told myself and everyone that I needed to be nearer the Mitchell Library for research purposes, and the house in Bearsden was too big and time consuming to look after, and I was getting into too comfortable a rut and it was affecting my writing. "A place like Bearsden is death to a working-class writer," I used to say. I even used to joke about having to move because I'd written a book about the place.

But looking back now, and struggling to be honest, did I not just move to be nearer my mother?

"One day," I used to say to her, "I'll make lots of money at my writing and I'll take you abroad on a holiday and you'll meet all sorts of new and interesting people and the sun will do you good."

(She had never been out of Britain in her life and, at this point, neither had I.)

But it was too late. She knew it and I knew it. She wasn't fit to get outside the Home eventually. I think that must have been when I moved house. I knew how terrible it was for a woman of my mother's temperament not to get out and about. Like me, she loved the pulsating life of the city, and as well as visiting me, there was nothing she liked better than a jaunt into town every day. The La Scala Restaurant was one of her favourite haunts. There, until she was no longer able, she often helped out as cashier when their regular cashier was off ill or on holiday or had left. It was like a second home to her and all the customers knew her. The public sitting-room of the YWCA was another of her regular ports of call.

"There's lonely, sad folk in the YW that depend on me to cheer them up," she used to say. "They'd miss me if I didn't go in and have a wee blether with them and give them a tune."

She always enjoyed a chat and laugh with Tommy, the old paper man at the corner of Sauchiehall Street and Hope Street too.

Once my mother couldn't get out, couldn't be independent, it was the beginning of the end for her. But her face lit up when I told her I'd found a flat near the home and could walk round and see her in ten minutes. I could see that she needed me to be near her to get reassurance from me. She seemed to pick anxiously at me all the time, searching out comfort. Her eyes would wilt with anguish and she'd say,

"Oh, Margaret, I hope Audley didn't think I didn't go in to see him sooner because I didn't want to see him. . . ."

I would assure her for the hundredth time that Audley had asked that she didn't come into the hospital at first because he didn't want her to be worried or upset. He loved her and would never think anything wrong about her.

She would gaze at me tragically and say:

"There was that time when he was a wee boy and I left your daddy and took Audley with me and I found out afterwards that Audley had German measles. Maybe that harmed his heart. Trailing him away like that instead of keeping him warm in bed."

Over and over again. I assured her that she'd been the best of mothers. No one could have been better.

"I kept remembering," she said, "how the poor soul suffered with the rheumatic fever."

And I reminded her that since that time he had been happily married, travelled abroad, and lived what life he'd had to the full.

"If only he hadn't been alone in that ward," she said.

125

She developed a fearful anxiety in case anything happened to me. I walked every day from the flat to visit her and she'd phone me beforehand to make sure I was coming. Afterwards she'd 'phone to make sure I'd arrived safely back.

"Don't go out at night," she'd say. "So many dreadful things can happen at night. The papers are full of them."

"Don't come the back way when you come to see me. Keep to the main street."

And so it went on. It was an almost intolerable irritation. I began to dread my daily visits. And yet I wanted to see her. I longed to reach out to her and be at one with her. How can I explain the undercurrent of conflict, the seething turmoil of emotion that prevented me? I cannot. Not even to myself. Although, as a writer, I've got to keep trying.

# CHAPTER TWENTY-THREE

MY FRIEND Ella was making me laugh recently. She was brought up in Balornock and remembered my mother from those days. Ella enjoys recalling old times.

"Remember," she said, "how your mother used to read teacups? She used to warn everybody that it was a lot of nonsense and she just did it for fun, but she was really good at it. My mother and I used to come round to your house and bring a bit of coal in our shopping bags because coal was rationed and my dad was the coalman, remember?"

It came back to me so vividly. My mother radiating pleasure at receiving the coal and immediately tossing it onto the fire and jabbing it about to make a cheery blaze. Then she'd fetch a pot of tea and a plate of gingersnap biscuits. We all had to take a biscuit and crack it against our elbows. According to my mother, if the biscuit broke in three pieces it meant we would get a wish.

After the cup-reading, she would say: "Now, come on through to the front room and I'll give you a wee tune."

She would make us all sing. Ella said the only time she ever sang in her life was in my mother's house. The same applied to me and I couldn't sing any better than Ella. I could never even remember any words. But my mother would never take no for an answer. I had to find a song book in the piano stool and sing words from that.

Ella laughed until tears poured down her face, remembering.

"She never worried about housework or unmade beds or anything like that, your mother. 'Och, the house will be here long after I'm gone,' she always said. 'Never mind the dirty dishes!' Then with a flourish on the piano, she'd close her eyes and launch with great feeling into — 'I think that I shall never see, a poem lovely as a tree. . . .'"

It was good recalling things like that. Happy things. Nights lying in bed with my wee brother in the darkness of the bedroom, listening to the reassuring sound of my mother's confident tread on the lobby linoleum as she went from living-room to kitchenette and back, getting my father's supper ready.

Knowing she was there.

I must lay the ghosts of other nights. Where was I? Who was that woman who bathed me in a zinc bath by the side of an old-fashioned black range? The room is a pool of shadows and I instinctively know it is far away from Glasgow. I see myself standing in the bath. The woman has gone out of the room. A man is sitting on a fender stool very close in front of me. There is something in the way he is staring at me. I remember his eyes with fear, even today. I lower my head, I see the vulnerability of my pink skin. I try to find some numb place inside my head where I'll see nothing and feel nothing.

Yet I sense that the woman has purposely left the room.

The shadows envelop me and I am in another room in a hole-in-the-wall bed. In the darkness, in the strange, unknown place, I wait in terror.

Someone once said that all great writing is a bonus that comes from an unhappy experience. I don't know about that. Everyone has had unhappy experiences at some time or other but not everyone writes, and of those who do, few produce great writing. Some of the world's greatest and most powerful books are badly written, if not from beginning to end, at least in parts.

Take *Wuthering Heights* by Emily Brontë as one example. I don't think anyone could deny that parts of that book are very badly written. It could be said that it is not even terribly original in plot or character. Heathcliff it has been claimed is reminiscent of Byronic and other heroes of "Gothic" fiction published before *Wuthering Heights*.

Nevertheless this story has a magic persuasive quality, a passion and power that classes it as one of the world's greatest books.

In my opinion it is such a wild and passionate book because between its covers is the wild and passionate spirit of Emily Brontë struggling to get out.

She may have appeared a shy, retiring little lady to her contemporaries but she was the same lady who, after telling her dog "Keeper" not to go up on the coverlet of her bed, dragged him down when he disobeyed and punched him between the eyes and kept on punching him until he was bleeding and half-unconscious.

There is a lot of theorizing and mystery surrounding the sadistic imagery in *Wuthering Heights*. It doesn't seem mysterious to me. Emily Brontë was simply writing with feeling, honest feeling, and her feelings included a powerful vein of sadism.

There are a great many academic theories about the morality of *Wuthering Heights*. It has been said that by directing our sympathies towards Heathcliff and by encouraging us to sympathize with Heathcliff and Cathy's rebellion, Emily Brontë wants us to oppose the order that oppressed them — conventional and orthodox morality — and that she creates another kind of morality in the book. I personally feel that Emily Brontë, sitting in Haworth

Parsonage writing the story of *Wuthering Heights* or striding across the moors thinking about Heathcliff and Cathy, wasn't working out any abstract theories of morality. I would bet my bottom dollar that nothing would be further from her thoughts.

When she thought about Heathcliff and he spilled over on to paper, *she* was Heathcliff and so she had a certain sympathy and understanding for his motivations and this naturally conveys itself to the reader. She would be Cathy too and when she made both Cathy and Heathcliff — especially Heathcliff — suffer later in the book, I believe Emily was at the mercy of a sado-masochism in her own nature.

This masochism was very evident in her life, especially towards the end of it when she cruelly punished herself and refused all offers of help. Her sister Charlotte wrote very worriedly of Emily to friends: .

> I fear she has pain in the chest, and I sometimes catch a shortness of her breathing. . . . She looks very thin and pale. . . . It is useless to question her: you get no answer. It is still more useless to recommend remedies; they are never adopted . . . she neither seeks nor will accept sympathy. To put any questions, to offer any aid, is to annoy; she will not yield a step before pain or sickness till forced; not one of her ordinary avocations will she voluntarily renounce. You must look on and see her do what she is unfit to do and not dare say a word. . . .

One day Emily got up and dressed as usual and began to sew. She sat sewing until her eyes were glazed and she was gasping for breath. By the time the doctor came that afternoon it was too late, Emily died at 2 o'clock.

That's the kind of person she was and that's why *Wuthering Heights* is the kind of book it is. In writing, it's the kind of person you are that matters. It's your own impact with life.

Writing techniques are something else. You've got to learn them and I believe you can learn them. Although Steinbeck says:

> If there's a magic in writing and I am convinced that there is, no one has ever been able to reduce it to a recipe that can be passed from one person to another. The formula seems to be solely in the aching urge of the writer to convey something he feels important to the reader. If the writer has that urge, he may sometimes but by no means always find the way to do it. . . .

They say everyone has at least one good book in them. I'm sure this is true. The challenge is in developing the characteristics necessary to write it. Many things go into the making of a novelist.

My brother made me a writer, and my father made me a writer, and perhaps most of all, my mother made me a writer.

I hear my friend Ella's laughter again:

"Do you remember how your mother could count up pounds, shillings and pence in her head with the speed of light? Yet she could never remember anybody's street number? It never bothered her though, did it? She used to address letters in all sorts of queer ways like: 'Mrs Smith, the house with the bird-bath in the garden, Cockmuir Street.' And it worked. Her letters always got there."

I remember. I remember my mother all ready to go out to play the piano at a very important function for which she was going to get paid. (She earned a few pounds that way when my father was off work with double pneumonia.) She was dressed in a long, bottle-green evening dress. God knows where or how she got it. But anyway, there she stood with proud dignity before us, back straight, handsome head held high, hands clasped in front of her waist displaying to advantage the delicate see-through sleeves with their patterns of coloured sequins. She wore no make-up. Her flushed cheeks and blue-black hair and brown eyes didn't need any enhancement.

She was beautiful.

How strange and confusing that my mother was younger then than I am now.

We laughed together, Ella and I, as if it had always been laughter. Yet still, in my mind's eye, there is the bent, old woman.

I went into the home one day and opened her bedroom door without knocking and saw her for a few seconds before she realized I was there. She was up and dressed waiting for me to come but sitting on the edge of the bed with her thin legs dangling. Utter hopelessness had drained her face and eyes and she was gazing bleakly, tragically into space.

The moment she saw me the spotlight turned on. She made a conscious effort to straighten her shoulders and lift up her head. She smiled and began chatting to me.

And all the time she clung to her desperate optimism. Each time she became ill she spoke of going to the hospital as if she was off on holiday to visit old and well-loved friends. (She did love the doctors and staff at that Homeopathic Hospital.) All she needed was a change of surroundings for a wee while, she would say, and everybody in the hospital was so nice.

But once in, she would hear people moaning and crying out in pain and dying and it would make her think all the more of Audley. All she needed, she would say then, was to get back to the Home among the old friends she'd made there. They were all so

130

nice, and she missed them. But when she got back to the Home, people were dying there too.

With each move she became frailer and weaker. And now she had angina as well as her other troubles. Then one day when I was kissing her goodbye, she clung round my neck and gazing up at me, said:

"If I could just stay a wee while at your place I'm sure that's all I need to put me right."

She'd always told everyone that I didn't want her to go into the home.

"There's always a welcome for me at Margaret's place," she'd say. "I didn't need to go into a home, you know. It was my idea, not Margaret's."

Sometimes she'd turn to me for confirmation and say: "Wasn't it?"

And I'd back her up with a firm: "Yes, of course." But it was all part of the act. I thought she knew it.

Now, for the first time, she put me to the test.

"Oh, no," I said. "I'd be afraid that you'd take one of your bad turns, Mummy, and I wouldn't know what to do to help you. You're far better here where there's the sick-bay and the nurses and Matron just along the corridor."

The light went out of her eyes. But she kissed me just the same.

I tried to make up for it on subsequent visits by becoming indignant when I learned that she hadn't a supply of tablets at hand to relieve her angina pain when it came on. My father used to always have some at hand so that when necessary he could melt one under his tongue. This relieved the angina spasm. My mother had to depend on someone hearing her cry out. I wanted to go along to the sick-bay and put things right but she was now in such an apprehensive, anxious state she didn't want to cause any trouble and made me promise not to mention a word about it.

She was very lucky, she said, having her bedroom so near to the sick bay, and everyone was really very nice.

By the time Christmas came and I told her that we'd collect her in the taxi and bring her out to our place for Christmas dinner, she wasn't able and instead had to spend Christmas Day in the sick-bay.

I went to see her. She wasn't in bed. One of the small wards had been cleared and the dozen or so women patients had been placed in a semi-circle in what looked like children's high chairs. Each had a tray fixed in front to pinion its occupant who was further immobilized with a blanket tightly trussed round legs and feet. Shawls had been tucked over hunched shoulders and ludicrous

131

paper crowns stuck on white heads.

Matron was going round untying bibs.

I looked at my mother. My beautiful, unique, courageous mother. Why did I not weep then? I weep now.

Matron said how they were all having a lovely party and they'd all been very good and eaten up all their dinner.

My mother said: "Margaret has a nice voice. She'll give you a song."

I would have given anything at that moment not to let her down, to have been able to please her and make her proud of me. But I just couldn't remember any words. I couldn't sing.

"Of course, you can," my mother said.

But I couldn't.

I don't think she believed me any more than she had believed my father. There was hurt and disappointment in her eyes but she managed to announce cheerfully, defiantly:

"Well, I'll give you a song."

She sang "Bless This House" and immediately Matron began distracting everyone's attention by fussing with the old lady in the next chair, pulling her up and saying loudly: "There you are, dear. That's better. That's a good girl."

For a moment my mother gazed round at the Matron but her sweet, clear voice did not falter. She sang to the end of her song.

After that she was returned to her bedroom and I visited her there every afternoon as usual except on the occasion when I went to see her in the morning because I'd promised to visit my Pakistani friends that afternoon.

"One day that terrible pain is going to take me away," she told me then. "But I'm not afraid of dying because it will mean I'll see Audley again." Her voice wavered a little. "Won't it?"

I willed absolute certainty into my voice and eyes.

"Yes, Mummy, you'll see Audley again. I know you will."

That was the last thing I ever managed to do for her. Later that afternoon I had a telephone call from the Home asking me to come at once. When I arrived and went hurrying along the corridor towards her room, I saw the nurse waiting for me outside her door.

My mother was dead.

They asked me if I wanted to look at her but I said, no.

Now I wish I had seen her, just once again.

Our tenement symphony is quiet now. All our old neighbours and friends, my brother, my father, my mother, they're all dead.

But I still have my writing. And, who knows, maybe the characters I write about will live on.

# Bibliography

Miriam Allott: *Novelists on the Novel*, Routledge & Kegan Paul.
John Braine: *Writing a Novel*, Eyre Methuen.
Joyce Cary: *Selected Essays* (ed. A.G. Bishop), Michael Joseph.
Christopher Derrick: *Reader's Report*, Gollancz.
Dianne Doubtfire: *The Craft of Novel-Writing*, Allison & Busby.
A. Hoffman: *Research*, Midas.
Arnold Kettle (ed.): *The Nineteenth-Century Novel*, Heinemann Educational Books.
Robert Liddell: *A Treatise on the Novel*, Cape.
Robert Lynd: *Books and Writers*, Dent.
Maxwell Maltz: *Psycho-Cybernetics*, Wiltshire Book Co.
W. Somerset Maugham: *The Summing Up*, Pan.
W. Somerset Maugham: *Ten Novels and Their Authors*, Mercury Books.
W. Somerset Maugham: *A Writer's Notebook*, Heinemann.
André Maurois: *The Art of Writing*, Bodley Head.
George Plimpton (ed): *Writers at Work — The Paris Interviews* (4th series), Secker and Warburg.
*The Secret Diary of William Byrd of Westover*, Arno Press.
*The Writers' and Artists' Yearbook*, Black.

# Index of Authors